Bitcoin For Financial Advisors

A Simple Manual For Understanding An Emergent Financial Instrument

Scott Dedels

Copyright © 2023 by Scott Dedels
All rights reserved.

"As an amusing thought experiment, imagine that Bitcoin is successful and becomes the dominant payment system in use throughout the world. Then the total value of the currency should be equal to the total value of all the wealth in the world. Current estimates of total worldwide household wealth that I have found range from $100 trillion to $300 trillion. With 20 million coins, that gives each coin a value of about $10 million."

Hal Finney, January 11, 2009

Contents

Introduction vii
    Take Bitcoin Seriously xii
    Proof of Work xiii
    About Advisors xiv
    Hard Money xvii
    Don't Be Peter Schiff xxi

What Exactly is Bitcoin? 1
    Bitcoin the Currency 3
    Bitcoin the Innovation 13
    Bitcoin the Network 17
    Bitcoin The Element 21
    Absolute Scarcity 26
    Don't Be Charlie Munger 33

Addressing Common Concerns 37
    Bitcoin Sentiment 37
    The Bitcoin Experiment Has Failed 38
    Bitcoin is a Ponzi 39
    The Greater Fool Theory 41
    The Price Cannot Go Up Forever 42
    Bitcoin is Right-Wing / Libertarian / Terrorist Financing / Black Market Money 45
    Bitcoin Undermines Fiat Currencies 46
    Cryptocurrency Bankruptcies 48
    Bitcoin is Unregulated 49

Future Innovations in Cryptocurrency Will Surpass
Bitcoin..51
Bitcoin is a Cult..53
Don't Be Frank Giustra...54

Finding a Place for Bitcoin 57
Appreciation VS Wealth Protection 58
Be Responsibly Long..60
Saving Your Money In Bitcoin...62
Fixed Income..64
Equities...66
Inheritance..67
Bitcoin ETFs Inside RRSP/ RESP/TFSA/LIRA etc..........68
As a Corporate Asset 70
Bitcoin Instead of Real Estate..71
Don't Be Peter Zeihan 74

Some Common Questions..77
Custodial Bitcoin VS Non-Custodial 77
Bitcoin VS Gold...78
Bitcoin VS the Bitcoin ETFs...79
Bitcoin VS Cryptocurrencies 80
Do I need to Buy a Whole Bitcoin?.....................................81
Dollar Cost Average or Lump Sum Purchase? 81
Don't Be Jim Rickards 82

The Case for Further Bitcoin Education 87

Introduction

"The root problem with conventional currency is all the trust that's required to make it work. The central bank must be trusted not to debase the currency, but the history of fiat currencies is full of breaches of that trust." Satoshi Nakamoto

Grasping Bitcoin can sometimes be both a blessing and a curse. It is an idea so powerful and inspiring that many for whom the light goes on have a hard time thinking about anything else. That definitely happened to me. To the bewilderment of my friends and family, seemingly overnight I became that guy almost unconsciously and unavoidably dropping into unsolicited conversations about hard money and Austrian economics.

I get obsessed with ideas when they make sense to me, and I have a history of adopting radical lifestyle changes when an idea in my mind becomes firm. I get that most people aren't wired this way. This pattern is something about me that is either endearing and quirky or really annoying. When the next thing for me became bitcoin, many people in my life just sort of took it as here we go again. Bitcoin as it happens is also that type of thing. People who don't understand it, really don't seem to care about it and you can always tell when someone moves from thinking they understand it, to actually understanding it. Because what happened to me happens to unsuspecting Bitcoiners all the time. A newfound compulsion to work it into every conversation possible.

I have worked in financial services since 2008, and started learning about bitcoin in the spring of 2020. Canada basically closed as a country that spring and at that time I was working at a large Insurance Brokerage as an Employee Benefits & Pension Plan Consultant. Before that, I was aware of bitcoin but had never looked directly at it. When our clients all had to close their doors simultaneously, our firm spent the early time of the lockdown becoming experts on the government's Covid aid strategies. In Canada, that was a time of unprecedented spending and money creation.

I didn't have an educational background in finance or commerce, and I felt I didn't know enough to have an opinion about what all this new government spending would mean. I was a history major at university, so I did have an understanding of the life cycles of empires, and the pivotal role that currencies have played in them. I started looking at dollars added to national balance sheets to fund the proposed aid packages and became curious about inflation, and I spent the early days of the pandemic reading university economics textbooks. From there, I somehow found my way to a book called *The Price of Tomorrow* written by a brilliant man named Jeff Booth. I credit Jeff with planting the Bitcoin virus in my brain, and I am forever grateful. I sure did take it on board. Six months after reading that book, I sold my house and used the proceeds to buy Bitcoin.

Bitcoin is, in some ways, a simple concept, but it is also highly esoteric and abstract. It solves a problem that almost everyone either doesn't realize exists or quite understands. Even the most educated experts in the financial sector do not understand bitcoin for the most part. In my fifteen-year career I have met top financial advisors from across the country. In my three years studying bitcoin, I have yet to meet another advisor who I would confidently say understands it. So today, we live in a bizarre time where most people – including those with the best understanding of financial markets – have not adequately grasped what Bitcoin's discovery means. Because of this, the appropriate everyday conversations around how it should be viewed in a portfolio, in my opinion are generally not happening.

Many people today feel that 'the system' is not working correctly or that central banks or governments are failing at their jobs. Inflation has crunched households all over the world. Energy and food price spikes have well exceeded whatever any major Western nation or news outlet reports inflation as. But very few people seem to have the time to look directly at the problem and try to understand what is happening. It's almost like people, in general, are just busy focusing on keeping their lives in order and doing what they can to stay ahead of rising costs and interest rate hikes. There is no extra time these days to step back and consider that there might be a systemic problem with how money works.

I think it fair to say that people study and learn much about how to grow money without spending time wondering precisely what money is and how it works. This may be because there was never much point in studying what money is because there were no viable alternatives and nothing to be done about it. Which makes a philosophical examination of money something of a useless thought exercise. The advent of Bitcoin has provided a reference point for bigger conversations about what money is and how it works.

The further I went down the Bitcoin rabbit hole, the more I learned exactly how many people are engaging in this intellectual conversation already. Bitcoin catalyzes new ideas about how money works and its societal role. Grasping Bitcoin concepts can be labor and time intensive, simultaneously making them tempting to dismiss. This is just as true for high-level money managers as for beginner investors. It is much easier to assume that Bitcoin is some kind of a joke or scam rather than spend however many hours it takes to assess the concept properly. I found Bitcoin attractive after around 50 hours. Still, it was probably more like after 500 hours before I started feeling grounded in the subject matter. I'm well over 1000 hours now and still learning things all the time.

500 hours? Well, I did mention I get obsessed. What can you possibly learn studying just bitcoin for that length of time? I get this question all the time. If you hold the position that Bitcoin is a ponzi, vaporware, internet fad it's easy to understand why rigorous bitcoin study would

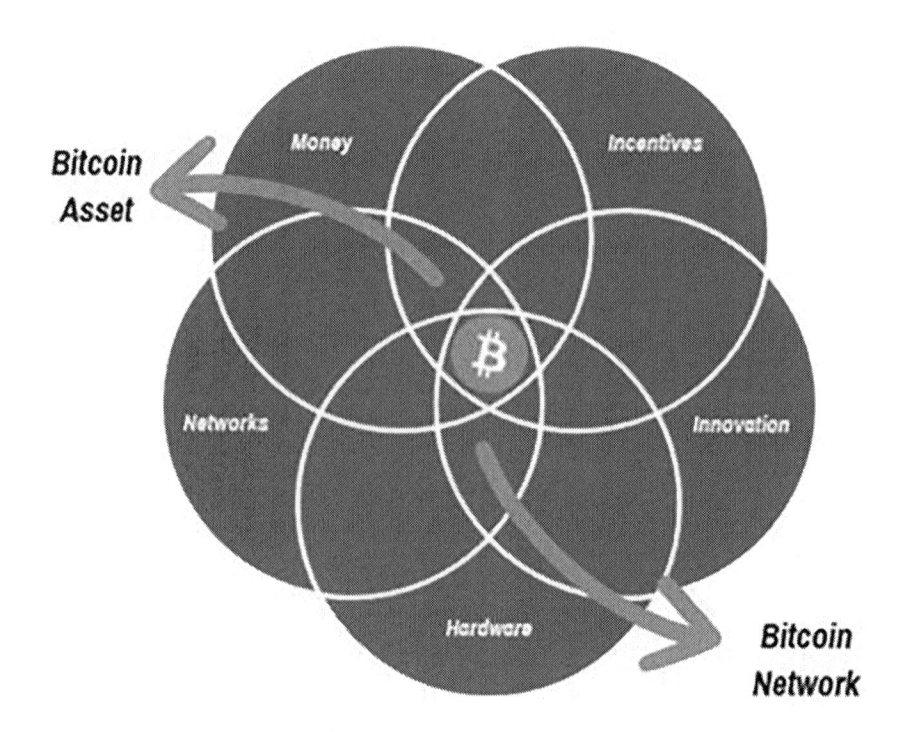

seem like a waste of time. Understanding bitcoin requires education in hard money, incentives, networks, and the technology that makes bitcoin unique. This foundation lays the groundwork for more extensive conversations about bitcoin and its potential trajectory as an asset class and its place in finance.

Bitcoin is the product of decades of intellectual endeavors, which sought to create peer-to-peer electronic cash, and beyond that a better form of money than what is currently used by most of humanity. A universally accepted, transparently finite asset, not beholden to any government or central bank. A borderless, native currency of the internet. The possibility of the separation of politics and money.

The lines between governments and banks have blurred increasingly since the creation of the US Federal Reserve in 1913, but particularly since the advent of 'too big to fail' in the wake of the 2008 meltdown. Fourteen years of continuous quantitative easing culminating with inflation reparation cheques issued in many places in 2022, should be a clear signal that in the western world banks and politics have entirely merged. Today we are bearing down on an even bigger change, Central Bank Digital Currencies. This technology will enable citizens to interact directly with their central bank, operating as an arm of the government- a universal federal tool for enforcement, surveillance, and central planning. Digital serfdom. As such, the possibility that technology could create separation between money and state makes bitcoin's mere existence have massive potential implications for the way the world works today and how it might in our increasingly digital future. It could very well be the most transformational technology of this century. Big statement. I tell people openly I believe bitcoin to be the most important discovery of our time. Something that will change the world even more than the internet did. That's usually where I get that look of "are we talking about the same thing?"

Most importantly, bitcoin is unlike anything that has come before it – that's the one thing I will tell anyone who will listen.

Take Bitcoin Seriously

"Fix the money, fix the world. It is really that simple."
Marty Bent

Understanding Bitcoin was made extra surreal by my largely overlapping social and professional circles. These were mainly composed of financial services professionals – many of whom quickly thought I had lost my mind. Once making sense, I assumed bitcoin would be easy to explain to people who understood financial markets better than I do. I have now talked to countless advisors, most of whom are very successful, about bitcoin. This book is informed by the reactions I have received in those interactions. In talking to advisors about bitcoin, I have observed that a sophisticated understanding of the financial system is not necessarily helpful in understanding bitcoin faster than the average person. Often the biases accompanying that knowledge can be a hindrance. In my experience many people who know next to nothing about bitcoin, have strong opinions about it being illegitimate, risky, or just flat out kooky.

What I experienced is consistent with the kind of narrative you tend to find in traditional financial media. Bitcoin is not something to be taken seriously. This could not be further from the truth, and if you accomplish only one thing in reading this book, my hope would be to at least dispel that notion.

While many colleagues think I'm nuts, I believe my contribution to the bitcoin movement is to translate some of my understanding of bitcoin into financial planning speak. Since understanding the core premises of bitcoin and what it might mean for financial services, I feel compelled to help advisors on a broad scale digest this big idea. I hope, from there, more competent and experienced people will take this concept where it needs to go – into the hands of the people trusting them with their financial futures.

Reading this book will hopefully give you at least an initial understanding of the depth and complexity of Bitcoin, the subject. I hope it will serve as a launch point for further Bitcoin learning, and the seeds of a feeling that bitcoin might be something that your clients should consider. Ideally upon completion you will be thinking about buying some bitcoin for yourself. What you will not find in this book is a detailed explanation of how Bitcoin, the technology works. I have purposely avoided this aspect of the conversation as it has been done very well already and my primary aim is to be as concise and simple as possible. At the end of the book, I have compiled a list of great resources should you be interested in more technical explanations.

Lastly, I say that nothing here is financial advice, and no one knows what the future holds. I have tried to write generally enough that advisors in the UK, Australia, the United States, or anywhere else this book lands will still find value. However, some aspects of the conversation pertain specifically to the Canadian financial system, with which I am most familiar.

Proof of Work

I have to wonder as well if the reason this exact book doesn't already exist is that earlier Bitcoiners who were also emersed in traditional finance have thought about it and deemed it a bad idea. I treat these bitcoin concepts with a high degree of reverence acknowledging that they take a big investment of time to understand. That means my attempt to explain them more succinctly probably increases the general chances of failure. I can say from personal experience (gathered leading up to this book) failure to correctly explain some bitcoin ideas can make them seem even more ridiculous to the person that didn't get it in the first place. I'm trying anyways but I think it's worth closing this by saying that for people who understand bitcoin, the worst thing you could do is something that would be akin to spreading bitcoin misinformation. We'll see how the Bitcoin community receives this book, if anyone ends up reading it. My personal take is that at the end of the day people who understand bitcoin have a responsibility to help other people understand it. It's a big responsibility and you want to do it right. Whether it was a good idea or not I wrote this book because I thought it needed to be written. Here goes.

About Advisors

"If you're a money manager you want to pretend that it's complicated to invest. If all you have to do is buy Bitcoin... all these people are out of business" Peter Thiel

I am a massive believer in the role financial advisors play. I started my career in financial services as a wholesaler for a major Canadian group insurance supplier. My job was to market our employee benefit plans to generalist financial advisors. I met a few hundred or so during that work for coffees and lunches. Most of those conversations were spent learning about their business and what made them tick. I have, in my career, met countless advisors. Mostly, I've been very impressed with the people who choose to take on the burden of creating and managing financial plans for everyone else. It's a big and important job that can also be mostly thankless.

My dad retired as a Mechanical Engineer in the spring of 2008. He had mostly worked for smaller oil field companies in Northern Alberta, and none offered a pension. Mom was diligent in building a culture of saving in our house, taking me to the bank to open my first savings account when I was 8. My parents planned ahead, maxing their RRSPs every year and setting aside what they could. Six months after retiring, the October financial crash wiped out 40% of what my parents had squirreled away throughout my dad's career.

About a year later, when I had been in my role for some time, I introduced my parents to the person who I thought was the best candidate I had met to manage their money. This was done after careful consideration. But my parents, like many, were outsiders to the financial world. Even with my urging, they were skeptical that this person I'd recommended would be any different than the advisor who had overseen their disastrous 2008. My dad, in particular, didn't want to be sold anything. After meeting the advisor I had chosen, my parents decided to move forward. Thirteen years later, they still credit that as the best thing I have done for them, and I tell this story all the time if people ask me about working with an advisor.

Financial advisors play a critically important role, helping people build plans so they can focus on doing what they enjoy instead of worrying about how they will pay for it. I do not see this going away. I do not believe AI and Robo-advisors will eliminate the human element of trust required to do this job right. Not anytime soon, at least.

I am assuming advisors will continue to play this key role during a time where I also expect bitcoin adoption will grow exponentially. I believe humanity to be in a time where bitcoin will crossover for the masses from fringe to mainstream, the same way the internet did in the late 90s. Bitcoin has roughly the same number of users the internet had in the late 90s, with a faster adoption curve, and in a time where ideas, in general, spread much more quickly. If this is correct, financial advisors will need to understand bitcoin sooner rather than later.

I would also argue that the conditions for bitcoin adoption today are more fertile than the world's latent demand for the world wide web at the turn of the century. I believe this primarily because of the escalating expansion of the global money supply that started in 2008 and accelerated greatly during 2020. Nearly everyone in the world today is being impacted by currency dilution. In 2000, very few were affected by being unable to shop online or stream video from their flip phones.

This book is a wake-up call for advisors who still think bitcoin is not something to be taken seriously. Financial advisors should play a vital role soon, helping people understand bitcoin and make informed decisions about incorporating it into their long-term plans. I don't have all the answers today, but if you are reading this book, it's likely you, on the other hand, do not have 500 hours to study bitcoin first. I hope this book's contents will get you thinking about bitcoin in a way that moves the conversation forward for you as a professional, and more ambitiously at an industry level.

Asymmetry of understanding, particularly concerning money matters, often creates defensive energy because the person who knows less never wants to be bamboozled. Advisors experience this with clients every day, but this applies to bitcoin as well, just with the shoe on the other foot. Often when I bring up bitcoin to advisors I can see them bristle. As you read this book, I want you to keep this in mind, the same way connecting with clients and prospects can often involve disarming that asymmetry of understanding. You are likely already aware of many arguments for why bitcoin won't work and is bad for your clients. Try to set those aside for now. This book is meant to help you understand what those arguments against bitcoin have ignored or failed to understand.

One final note – Bitcoin is a living idea. Many of these ideas are not my own; they represent the ongoing conversation in the Bitcoin community. I constantly listen to other Bitcoiners, too many to catalog and credit. While reading this, should you find that I have presented an idea you credit as yours; please consider this the highest form of flattery. The bitcoin conversation has exposed me to many brilliant people of whom I am constantly in awe. I consider it a personal honor to repackage some of those great ideas for whoever else might take them on and grow them even more. This is one of the greatest aspects of the bitcoin community.

Hard Money

"It is well enough that people of the nation do not understand our banking and monetary system, for if they did, I believe there would be a revolution before tomorrow morning." – Henry Ford

Money is a tool that allows societies to move away from bartering. As a technology, the invention of a medium of exchange allows for complex trade and the accumulation of wealth. Money's job is to serve as a mechanism for transferring value. A core feature of money being good at its job is its ability to store that value when it is not changing hands.

An asset's hardness refers to that asset's ability to retain its value over time. By extension, hard money is money that retains its value or purchasing power over time. Almost no one alive today has lived in a society where money is remotely hard. The government money, or 'fiat' that we all earn and save in, has proven to be a very poor store of value, much more than most people can comprehend. For example, the Canadian dollar has lost roughly 96% of its purchasing power since 1915.[1]

The inflation problem has become so normalized for almost everyone participating in society that very few people view it as a non-mandatory aspect of how economies work. This especially includes financial services professionals whose job is making money work instead of wondering how it works. Inflation can be viewed as a result of soft money, or currencies' inability to retain their value over time. At this point, the idea of target inflation has become so engrained in economic logic that it is essentially systemic brainwashing. We have all been successfully convinced that money losing its purchasing power over time is a necessary and useful feature of healthy economies. So much so that we generally don't see debate on whether or not it is even proven necessary.

Think about that for a second. Most people acquire the money they have by working for it. That effort earns a reward, and we store that reward in money until we do something else with it. If that money cannot effectively store that reward, it is basically wasting your efforts. That poorly stored monetary value does not merely evaporate into

---

[1] "Canada Inflation Calculator." In2013Dollars.com. Accessed March 31, 2023. https://www.in2013dollars.com/Canada-inflation.

the ether. It is confiscated by currency dilution. When new money is created out of thin air, it reduces the value of all the money that existed previously. The money that you worked hard to earn, or the work you performed to earn it, is made less valuable every time the money supply is expanded.

Soft currency changes the risk calculation of everything we do in life. It invalidates saving as a viable long-term strategy and, as a result, consumerizes us all. We constantly spend money in exchange for assets or useless things, and we do this not because we explicitly understand that money is losing its value but because we all know that prices rise over time. Asset prices rising is your reason for taking risks in investing. Prices going up is your reason for purchasing today instead of waiting. This is all rooted in soft money. When your money cannot hold its value over time, doing nothing with it is not an option.

Countries are in the same predicament that we are as individuals. Expansion of the supply of US dollars has exported destructive inflation to much of the developing world. Since 1970, the external public debt of developing countries has increased from $46 billion to $8.7 trillion USD.[2]

Rising asset prices make it harder for the asset poor to get ahead, which traps many in positions where wealth accumulation takes a back seat to survival. When money does not hold its value, we become slaves to it. This is just as true for lower-class people as for developing nations. Inflation is a system that inherently penalizes those with less.

---

[2] "IMF and World Bank Repress Poor Countries." Bitcoin Magazine, December 14, 2018. https://bitcoinmagazine.com/culture/imf-world-bank-repress-poor-countries.

There has never been a tool to imagine an entirely different way of commerce for everyone. Hence, people spend their time thinking about maximizing the opportunity they have in the current system instead of how things could be completely different. An entirely different system might seem ridiculous at a cursory glance, but there are several historical examples of societies where money has been much harder. Hard money and prosperity have been closely linked where it has been allowed to exist. The best discussion of this topic I have seen can be found in Saifedean Ammous's *The Bitcoin Standard*. Saifedean is a master Bitcoiner, and if you are interested in a deeper understanding of the history of money and how we got here, I would start there.

The bitcoin argument, in a nutshell, is that currencies are systematically diluted without express public consent. The process is not transparent regarding the rate and volume at which new money is issued. The opaque nature of this process confuses price signals in free market economies and forces spending and risk-taking while simultaneously penalizing saving. Currency dilution forces us all onto a hamster wheel. All participants in the current system are racing to grow their money at a rate that outpaces how fast it is losing value. It also is a system that has been proven throughout history to morally corrupt most people the closer they are to the creation of new money. Inflationary money has, throughout history, inevitably consolidated most of the wealth in the hands of a few. Diluting money incentivizes an 'every person for themselves attitude.' As asset prices rise in concert with diminishing purchasing power, those without assets have an increasingly difficult time accumulating any meaningful wealth. Those with assets are compelled to get their hands on whatever they can.

Most importantly, the inflationary monetary system is built on a bedrock of credit and debt. Both have been tools for prosperity and economic growth. Still, debt growth inevitably becomes a terminal illness for expanding fiat currencies. This transpires when the ratio of debt and actual economic activity becomes so out of whack that productivity can no longer service debt. Instead, when this point arrives, money printing is used to service debt, diminishing the nominal value of that debt at the expense of the currency's purchasing power. This is where we are today, at a point where most countries will be forced to issue new money to service existing debt, until one by one, they all default on their debt that can never be repaid.

Bitcoin offers the prospect of a global currency that cannot be diluted and is issued at a transparent and fixed rate. It is entirely foreign to how everything works today, which is why so many people struggle to see value in bitcoin or what value owning bitcoin has. It is a solution to the problem that almost no one realizes even exists – that our entire way of running economies and governments is built on a system that continually devalues money, surreptitiously confiscating wealth, and consolidating it in the hands of the few.

Don't Be Peter Schiff

> "The FTX bankruptcy proves the entire [Bitcoin] rally was a fraud. It will never be repeated. Bitcoin mania is over." – Peter Schiff

Ideas new to us are understood in two ways – either assimilated or accommodated. New ideas are assimilated when they fit into our existing paradigms of how things work. New ideas are accommodated when we must carve out new room for that idea that does not fit neatly into what we already know. If you haven't guessed yet, bitcoin falls into the latter. That bitcoin must be accommodated is partly why I feel financial services professionals can be disadvantaged in onboarding bitcoin ideas. They already have a high degree of understanding of other financial instruments and how they work, like equities, gold, bonds, and real estate. So, there is a strong tendency to want to assimilate it, sweeping it into existing paradigms. I have commonly witnessed the predisposition to view bitcoin by categorizing it purely as an asset like every other asset – which technically it is. However, with that comes bias, acknowledged or not. It tends to obscure the deeper consideration that Bitcoin might be a new type of asset with a mix of properties that make comparing it to previous alternatives a futile exercise. When an understanding of bitcoin is sought by comparing it to other kinds of investments, bitcoin becomes almost impossible to comprehend. As a result, grokking how it might fit into a financial plan will be an equally impossible feat.

Accommodating can also be uncomfortable; it requires much more work than assimilation and may force the consideration of larger questions. You might even find that, while you read this book, your reaction to a triggering statement will be to either dismiss it or want to disprove it. Understanding that not everyone is up for accommodating bitcoin has been a significant learning for me, and I feel it requires special mention. Entering this book and understanding finance likely means you will need to do some accommodating to successfully grasp the content.

Ask any client of Peter Schiff – the world's most notorious anti-bitcoin money manager. Schiff passed on Bitcoin at USD10 and has dug his heels in favor of gold ever since. During that time, Bitcoin was the best-performing asset ever, while the price of gold in that same period was basically flat. Schiff could have been the most outstanding asset manager of all time. However, instead, his bias prevented (and still prevents) him from seeing bitcoin for what it is. His paradigm is that bitcoin is fool's gold in cyberspace without any of the benefits of the physical metal. This bias is common to gold bugs. You can't make Bitcoin into jewelry or hold one in your hand, so in some way, it will never be as valuable as gold. Evaluating bitcoin as it compares directly to gold is the most obvious way to contextualize the problem by assimilating bitcoin as an idea.

Schiff is also a great example of someone whom traditional finance takes seriously. At the same time, the much smaller Bitcoin community tends to engage him on social media but essentially regards him as a fool for holding so tightly onto opinions deeply rooted in not understanding the technology and true value proposition.

The other common challenge for advisors understanding bitcoin is trust in the system. Most financial advisors thrive in the industry when they believe their work is helping people. They make a living by convincing people to participate in the existing financial system and maximizing it. Bitcoin has the potential to disintermediate existing institutions and shines an unfavorable light on central banking. This matters — if money itself is broken, it stands to reason that every product built to maximize the growth of that money is also likely broken. Some aspects of looking deeper at bitcoin could trigger advisors who might have to consider that the advice they gave clients in good faith might be wrong. I fondly joke that most advisors have the same trust in the financial system that realtors have in real estate. (This is the topic of a separate book, but I believe Canadian real estate to be one of most inappropriately overvalued asset classes in the entire world). This is not to disparage realtors or advisors. The point is you need to believe in what you sell, and often, that belief magnetizes clients to an advisor because what people are buying is the plan. I would guess most advisors will agree that it is more important to have a plan at all, rather than for example what specific mutual funds your advisor selected for you.

The good news is you are still early; most of the world still does not understand bitcoin. Overcoming established trust in the system concerning the appropriate consideration of bitcoin is a big one to bite off. While the network grows in the number of participants, bitcoin's risk/reward proposition improves. At USD20,000, it is considerably less risky than it was at USD1000 because of the evolution and growth of the network and the changes in global financial conditions which have happened during that time. The combination of inherent system trust and the difficulty in accommodating Bitcoin as an idea can be linked easily to most of the familiar anti-Bitcoin tropes. I will address this later.

As you continue reading, please take the information offered at face value. The journey to understanding Bitcoin takes most people much longer than 30 minutes (or however long it will take you to read this book). The goal here is to reframe bitcoin and provide a structure for you to research more if you choose and build an informed opinion on what it is and its value. Should you wish to properly understand Bitcoin, further study will certainly be required.

What Exactly is Bitcoin?

"Bitcoin can be best understood as distributed software that allows for transfer of value using a currency protected from unexpected inflation without relying on trusted third parties." – Saifedean Ammous

Bitcoin is a network where strangers can exchange value online without counterparty risk or needing a middleman such as a bank or a payment company. Bitcoin can also be considered the medium of exchange on that network.

Bitcoin is the world's only decentralized currency not issued by a government or central bank. It is an asset whose scarcity is verifiable and whose issuance is programmed to become even more rare over time. There are only 21,000,000 Bitcoin, and that is all there will ever be. The current price of roughly USD 20,000 makes it the 26th largest currency in the world. It is money that can be transacted peer to peer without an intermediary. No bank or payments company is required. No one party influences its monetary policy, which is permanently etched in digital stone.

Beyond all of that, Bitcoin is also:

- the world's only entirely community-driven, independent currency
- a monumental innovation in accounting and transacting
- an extremely viral growing network
- the world's scarcest and first man-made commodity
- the best-performing asset ever

It is the best-performing asset over a ten-year period. It is the fastest to reach a valuation of USD 1 trillion in human history.[3] No matter how you slice it, Bitcoin has provided incredible returns for just about everyone willing to hold for at least four years.

Regarding bitcoin, do not confuse its novel nature with its not being a serious endeavor. One thing I tell every advisor I meet, bitcoin is no longer a curiosity – we are only still very, very early. Understanding this was a huge shock for me. Many people seem to have the idea that bitcoin is still a gimmick. It has been a long time since it was anything remotely fringe.

Bitcoin conferences happen routinely worldwide, attracting huge crowds and bright minds. The world's largest institutions, including Fidelity, Mastercard, PayPal, and JP Morgan, are holding Bitcoin or building products and services around it. A nation-state, El Salvador has adopted it as a legal tender; and is accumulating Bitcoin on its federal balance sheet. It is a system that is snowballing in users across all continents. Many billionaires openly hold Bitcoin today – including Peter Thiel, Ray Dalio, and Tim Draper. In April of 2022, Mexican

---

[3] "Bitcoin Becomes the Best-Performing Asset of the Decade." Yahoo! Finance, December 31, 2019. https://finance.yahoo.com/news/bitcoin-becomes-best-performing-asset-132208120.html.

billionaire Ricardo Salinas announced 60% of his liquid assets were held in Bitcoin.[4]

So how does an instrument like this carve out a position in financial planning? Before we worry about that, let's start by addressing these claims individually.

Bitcoin the Currency

"Abundance in money equals scarcity in everything else" – Jeff Booth

Money is a technology that allows economies to become more complex. It allows for trade to occur instead of barter. Before the invention of money, if someone wanted milk and had only turnips to offer, the only way they could get milk was if someone with milk wanted turnips. Money allows the turnips, or the energy of the work that produced the turnips, to be turned into value. So, money is a technology that stores and transfers work or energy in the form of value.

Fiat currency is where the government sets that value so that parties exchanging money instead of bartering do not have to verify the value of the medium of exchange. It is the government's promise that serves as the foundation of the deal.

---

[4] Mozee, Carla. "Mexican Billionaire Ricardo Salinas Pliego Says He Has Liquidated His Entire Portfolio to Invest in Bitcoin." Business Insider, April 20, 2022. https://markets.businessinsider.com/news/currencies/bitcoin-mexican-billionaire-liquid-portfolio-ricardo-salinas-pliego-crypto-investment-2022-4.

As I mentioned in the previous chapter, one way to look at the dilution of fiat currencies is that continuous expansion makes them a poor store of energy. The stored energy of your money is best expressed through purchasing power. Constantly expanding currencies have seen purchasing power diminish consistently over time. The unproven notion that inflation is good or required is broadly hard-coded into how most people view money. In the modern financial system, the trade we all make in exchange for our purchasing power over time is that asset prices tend to increase along with the prices of everything else. This gives people the notion that the price of everything going up forever is ok as long as the price of things you own or sell goes up faster than the price of the things you want to buy. That way, everyone has the false sense that they are 'getting richer' or setting themselves up for the future. This is the essence of the rat race.

How do we know that money, being a sound energy store, is inherently better than the current system? Dilutionary fiat currency extracts value from the producing level of the economy by creating new money out of thin air that does not require any work. The new cash diminishes the value of all existing money, skewing the relationship between work and money unfavorably for those doing the work. The endless creation of new money can endlessly diminish existing money's value. This is the core aspect of inflation brainwashing that Bitcoiners have rejected. In today's raging inflation environment, the stated goal of Western Central Banks is to get inflation back to target. That people are begging for this shows precisely how entrenched this idea is. Essentially, as a society, we are fine with stealing the value of our work via the dilution of the money we earn. So long as it is done slowly enough that it does not make the hamster wheel, we are all on too hard to spin.

Hard money cannot arbitrarily be created out of thin air. This is the core premise of Bitcoin. Hence, the Proof of Work consensus mechanism on which the Bitcoin network runs. New Bitcoins are not created out of thin air. They are produced through an energy-intensive and highly competitive computational process called mining. Bitcoins are issued at a fixed and declining rate through this provable computational work. The more people want to participate in mining, the more difficult Bitcoins become to mine. Adding more miners cannot speed up production. There is no way to hack the creation of new Bitcoin and make it easier. Users of Bitcoin have agreed on the importance of money not having a limitless supply and being created at the whim of a human being. Bitcoin, the currency, has firm rules which can never be changed. It makes Bitcoin the first time humanity as a species has had the promise of using a form of money that cannot be arbitrarily diluted without consent.

The permanently fixed supply of Bitcoin is not an obvious homerun utility for most people who:

1. Do not understand the current state and history of the expansion of the money supply
2. Do not understand the predicament central banks are presently in concerning, most likely, having to continue to expand that supply.

Instead, Bitcoin skeptics love to point to its price performance over the 12 months, starting from the most recent cycle top in November of 2021. This was when Bitcoin saw a nearly 70% tumble in price while inflation was skyrocketing. For many critics this cemented failure as protection against inflation.

There is a crucial distinction to make between the short-term fluctuations in Bitcoin's current price in dollars or euros, and the price movements of basically every other thing you can realistically own. ***Whatever portion of Bitcoin you can purchase, taken as a percentage of the total amount of Bitcoin available, can never change – regardless of the price in dollars for which Bitcoin is trading.*** There is no other currency on earth that offers this promise. For this reason, it is more accurate to view the current Bitcoin price as the minimum price the market is willing to sell Bitcoin, not the maximum price for which someone will buy it. Every single Bitcoin circulating is owned. When you buy Bitcoin, you are buying it from someone else willing to sell it.

What, instead, can you buy with a fiat currency? The value of the Canadian dollar can be expected to reduce over time as the total number of Canadian dollars continually expands. This is independent of the fluctuating price of Bitcoin in Canadian dollars – but keep in mind that every currency except Bitcoin expands continuously over time. That means over long periods, there will, in theory, only be more and more fiat money available to chase the same amount of Bitcoin. It also means every single fiat currency user in the world is in the same predicament.

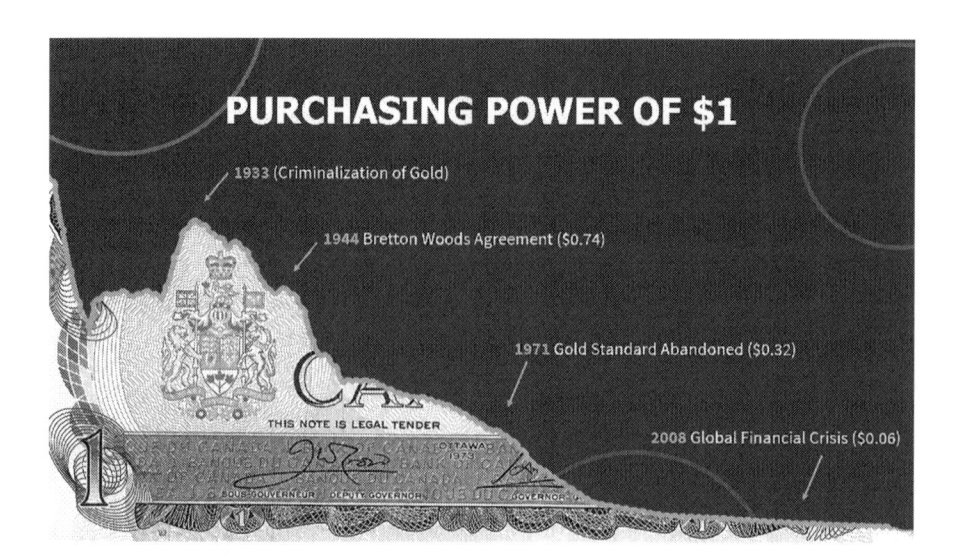

PURCHASING POWER OF $1

1933 (Criminalization of Gold)

1944 Bretton Woods Agreement ($0.74)

1971 Gold Standard Abandoned ($0.32)

2008 Global Financial Crisis ($0.06)

Bitcoin offers protection against inflation for those who understand the solution is to exit inflating currencies rather than try to outrun them. To understand how, divorce bitcoin's power as a store of financial energy from its short-term price movements in money. This is probably the single most challenging bitcoin concept to grasp, particularly for people in financial services who are used to measuring simple performance. Buy low, sell high, and make a profit. Bitcoin is built to run differently than all the other monetary networks worldwide. It is a closed system that traps energy by design. Debasement can go on for a long time, but eventually, it leads to collapse.

Every single fiat currency in human history has ultimately succumbed to debasement. We know how the fiat experiment ends; it has already ended many times.

Many people who own Bitcoin do not understand this, which is why people who bought at USD69,000 will sell at USD20,000. That decision is made from a place of still measuring the worth of Bitcoin in fiat money. Bitcoin will harden as the number of holders who understand this mechanism grows as a percentage of the total holders. This is also why we are still very early in the process. While there are many valid reasons to do it, selling bitcoin for fiat money is exchanging something finite for something infinite. You're jumping on to a moving train. The bitcoin you sold might be worth more fiat money than when you bought it, but that fiat money probably has also diminished in value during that same time, obscuring the real profit.

A challenge with discussing complex topics like this in a brief overview is the risk of oversimplification. I understand there are more factors required for understanding inflation than the total circulating supply of money. The point is that Bitcoin represents an alternative protection against inflation via debasement because it is a better energy store than fiat currency. The supply can never dilute.

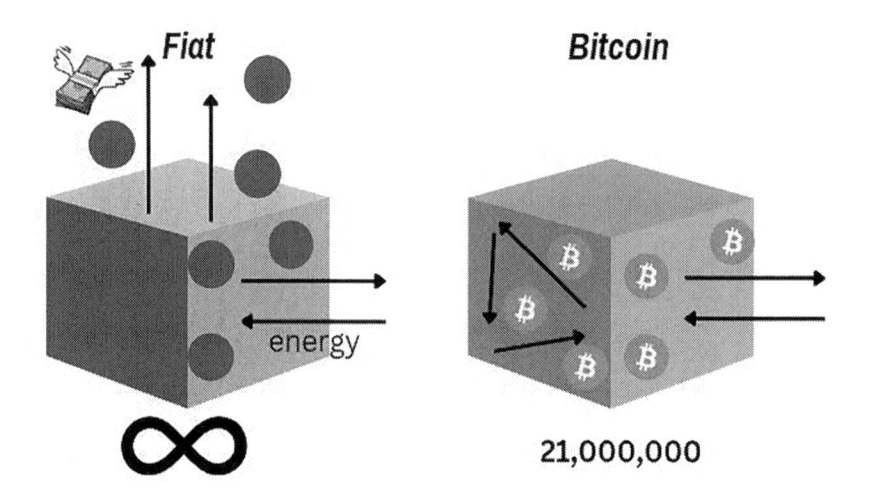

Fiat

energy

∞

Bitcoin

21,000,000

As a species, we have never had free market competition in money. As a result, money is one of the very few lasting technologies where innovation and performance have not been required for survival. For the most part, governments have enjoyed a monopoly on the control of money, which could easily be argued has been anti-competitive in terms of creating a market for innovation and improvement in the way money works. The term fiat comes from the Latin meaning 'let it be done,' which basically means use this money or else – not exactly what you might call a bedrock for innovation. Bad money benefits those who are in control of creating it. This is called the Cantillon effect, which states that inflation most benefits those closest to the spigot of new money created and penalizes those furthest away.[5] Inflation is a

---

[5] "What Is the Cantillon Effect and Why It's Even More Important Now." Sovereign Wealth Fund Institute, June 1, 2021. https://www.swfinstitute.org/news/89070/what-is-the-cantillon-effect-and-why-its-even-more-important-now.

hidden tax, a means for surreptitiously confiscating wealth under the guise of business as usual. In medieval Europe, wars were pre-funded with taxes collected, and the fighting often stopped when the money ran out. In the fiat world, wars are funded by creating money out of thin air. Having money based only on a government's promise removes for the government the pesky need to collect the money required to do anything. Instead of demanding a contribution directly, creating new money at the source requires no permission and simply costs existing holders of that money their purchasing power. Done right, the process is just gradual enough that no one, for the most part, gets upset, and this is why we have a Bank of Canada target inflation of 2%. Ever wonder why we have an inflation target from central banks? Saifedean recently quipped, "If 2% inflation is better than 0%, why is 4% not better than 2%?" I would love to hear a good answer.

Bitcoin is a serious endeavor trying to solve a problem few people understand. It is built to outcompete fiat money by rewarding users with the benefits of hard money. Before the discovery of Bitcoin, the technology to cause free market competition of money did not exist. This is part of why the idea of Bitcoin itself can be strange. You might find the concept of non-state money weird, which is why many disregard Bitcoin's innovation as a currency. However, then you vastly underestimate historical examples where new predators were introduced into environments where prey did not have sufficient time to adapt and evolve. This happened famously to the Dodo bird on the island of Mauritius, which never developed the ability to fly and was quickly hunted to extinction when Europeans arrived suddenly. It did not have time to adapt and as a result had little chance to survive. Much like the Dodo bird, fiat currencies have never evolved to face a predator, and without an abundance of time to adapt they may suffer the same fate.

Bitcoin, the currency, is built on game theory. Understanding this simple premise leads many Bitcoiners to believe that, beyond merely growing as an asset in time, we will see an inversion where Bitcoin emerges as the world's dominant monetary network. The more you know about Bitcoin, the less crazy this idea sounds. One day, instead of bitcoin being priced in dollars or euros, everything else will be priced in bitcoin. How would that work? From a game theory perspective, the existence of one viable sound money places all money users in a prisoner's dilemma. A prisoner's dilemma is a decision-making matrix that puts strangers in a competition where cooperation produces the most favorable outcome for all, and betrayal creates the most significant penalty.[6]

In the context of Bitcoin, we consider either individuals or societies one by one having to decide between cooperating using Bitcoin or continuing to use their inflationary and censorable government-issued currencies. Government-issued currencies will penalize nearly all users over time. In this framework, the failure or delay of bitcoin adoption creates the least favorable outcome for all. Should bitcoin fail, humanity will continue down an endless planned path of currency devaluation and the inevitable concentration of wealth in a smaller and smaller segment of the ultra-elite.

In the example below, we consider Central banks. Inflation, when severe, is a politically destabilizing force that, if extreme enough, can cause regime collapse. In the first world we complain about rising prices, in less fortunate places money has become worthless, sometimes overnight. The Bitcoin dilemma will apply to Central banks at whatever rate inflation creates political instability in their country and the relative

---

[6] "Prisoner's Dilemma." Wikipedia. Accessed January 2nd, 2023. https://en.wikipedia.org/wiki/Prisoner%27s_dilemma.

prosperity seen in Bitcoin-adopting countries elsewhere- likely starting in places where currency value has the worst track record. Today those countries can either devalue their currencies by accepting predatory loans from the IMF and the World Bank, or consider an alternative return to hard money either with Bitcoin, or commodities backed money.

Suppose that Central banks in poorer parts of the world adopt sound money incrementally and sound money is proven to be a net positive where it is adopted. In that case, it stands to reason that other nations and Central banks will be forced to consider the same decision when inflation inevitably becomes pressing for them as well. This experiment has started with El Salvador and its neighboring countries in Central America are watching closely.

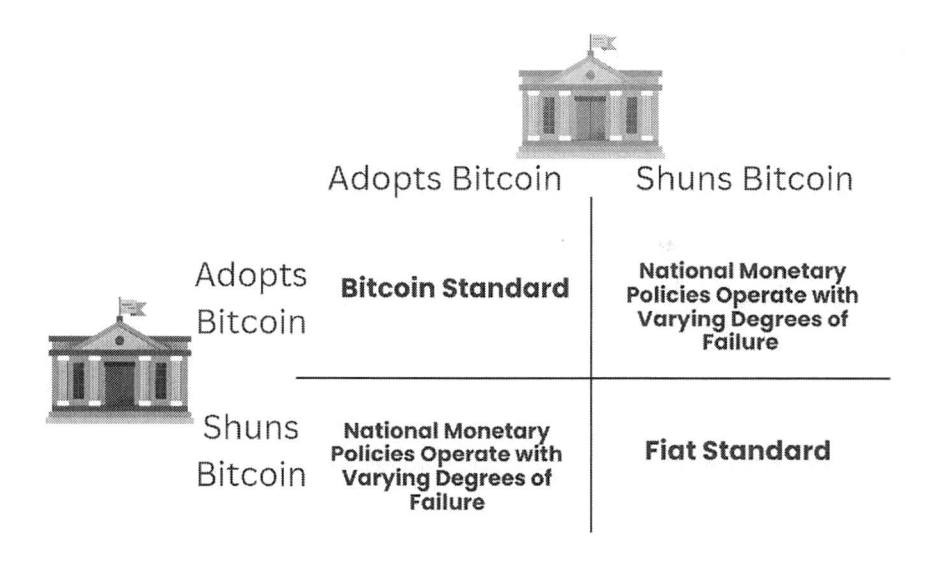

	Adopts Bitcoin	Shuns Bitcoin
Adopts Bitcoin	**Bitcoin Standard**	National Monetary Policies Operate with Varying Degrees of Failure
Shuns Bitcoin	National Monetary Policies Operate with Varying Degrees of Failure	**Fiat Standard**

The idea exists that Governments will never willingly cede the power to control their currencies. However, this ignores the fundamentals of the prisoner's dilemma, which has proven that positive outcomes are a sound basis for expectations of cooperation in environments where participants have access to equal information. Another common suggestion is that countries will sooner unite to globally ban bitcoin, than be forced to adopt it. This assumes a level of cooperation between competing countries that we don't have much precedent for. Geo-politics is a complex game, and it is entirely possible adversarial states could view bitcoin as a strategic tool worth embracing. A partial global ban or regional ban, where escape hatches exist create negate this strategies viability. A regional bitcoin ban could backfire something like how Soviet communism imploded trying to outspend Western capitalism.

Ban ideas also ignore many realities of Bitcoins uncensorable nature, which we will discuss later. Suppose this game theory proves to be accurate at a nation-state level. In that case, grass roots political will could eventually be strong enough to force cooperation among banks as a survival strategy taking the decision to adopt bitcoin out of the hands of the bankers and politicians

How would this play out? It starts with El Salvador prospering. Spiraling debt could easily cause other developing nations to look at the El Salvadorian model and think it's worth a try. Say the number of Central Banks using a Bitcoin standard grows. The more countries that succeed with bitcoin, the more pressure other countries will have to participate. Because of bitcoins capped supply, the more people who use it, the higher the price will go. The countries choosing to ignore hard money and pursue ongoing currency dilution instead will see the value of their expanding currencies move farther and farther away from digitally transparent and scarce money being used by the bitcoin banks. It is a matter of finite versus infinite. Inflation can continue endlessly. A good analogy might be flooring the gas pedal when your car is stuck in the snow. At a certain point, regardless of how fast the tires are spinning, it stops helping and eventually can make the vehicle more stuck.

The longer that Bitcoin does not go away, and the more people that start to interact with and use it, the more people will understand how it works and what it means – creating a broader symmetry of information. This is the Lindy effect, which states that the longer non-perishable items survive, the better their chance of long-term survival becomes. Ideas are viral in the same way that technologies are. Today very few people understand what bitcoin means, and despite that, it has thrived. Why would the world's population still choose to use inferior government money once a large portion of them understand that a more egalitarian alternative exists? And that is an alternative where the value of money is not at the whim of politicians and bankers. It's worth wondering. Bitcoin's superior ability to store wealth relative to all fiat currencies suggests fiat currencies will struggle to compete with its intrinsic value, and it could eventually achieve a network effect in money. We will revisit this concept in greater depth in the coming sections. For now, it's a fascinating thought experiment. And it's an authentic potential scenario with a decent chance of playing itself out in the not-too-distant future.

Bitcoin the Innovation

> *"If you want to compare Bitcoin to something else, compare it to fire, the number zero, the wheel, the printing press, or electricity."* Gigi

Accounting started in ancient Sumeria some 5000 years ago when clay tablets were baked in the sun to form the world's first transaction records or receipts. This is single-side accounting – the record of a sale. In 1494 double-sided accounting was born, and since we have had a record for buyers and sellers. This is why we have accountants today, whose job is to make sure, among other things, that both sides of the ledger add up. Double-sided accounting led to a whole new sophistication of banking and commerce. It made transactions more complex than two parties exchanging money and goods or services. Five hundred years later, this innovation has greatly benefited society. However, most do not recognize its Achilles heel, its point of failure – the need for an intermediary, the recordkeeper of that ledger.

Bitcoin represents the third stage in the evolution of accounting. The actual innovation is a confluence of technologies the Bitcoin protocol successfully combined. Among these innovations are the distributed ledger that the Bitcoin network records transactions on and the proof of work consensus that provides a robust defense against malicious actors who might try to submit fraudulent transactions or gain control of the network. The intention here is to avoid getting overly technical – there are plenty of technical manuals on how Bitcoin works.

The Bitcoin network is designed to function based on a community-maintained consensus that the transactions being processed are correct. Everyone participating in the network has the common goal of perfection on transactions because fraudulent transactions would simultaneously destroy the value of everyone's assets. Because of this built-in honor system, participants exchanging Bitcoins need not worry if the bitcoins they receive are legitimate. Transactions on the Bitcoin network are irreversible, which removes an additional degree of risk for merchants, particularly in online retail.

Without verifying the authenticity of the currency being used as a medium or proving that funds exist, users also do not need an institution in the middle to act as recordkeeper. This means faster settlement – Bitcoin transactions settle in about 10 minutes. With lower fees – Bitcoin has moved Billions of dollars for pennies. While we still use cash today, most payments are processed by companies like Visa and Mastercard, which charge exorbitant fees for their service- as high as 8% in the developing world. This is not to mention the banks who charge you for the right to loan the money you deposit to them at 9 or 10 times multiple. Want to wire transfer money internationally? Companies like Western Union will charge you up to 20% and take days to do it. The Bitcoin network is already moving massive volumes of money. In 2022 already, over 8T USD was using Bitcoin- that's $260,000USD per second. Think about that for a second.[7] Over 8 trillion dollars in 2022 alone has been moved worldwide without a bank.

But perhaps the most critical application for this innovation is not in disintermediating traditional financial institutions – but instead in providing many of the services they offer today to people all over the world who do not have access to conventional banks.

According to a worldbank.org report from July 2022, the number of unbanked people in the world is 1.4 billion.[8] These people cannot store and accumulate the energy from their labor. Without the ability to store and accumulate wealth, unbanked people have little real hope of lifting themselves out of poverty. Today all over the world, anyone with a cell phone and the internet can download a Bitcoin wallet and start storing

---

[7] Finbold. (2022, January 5). Over $8 Trillion Worth of Transactions Made on Bitcoin Blockchain in 2022. https://finbold.com/over-8-trillion-worth-of-transactions-made-on-bitcoin-blockchain-in-2022/#:~:text=Over%20%248%20trillion%20worth%20of%20transactions%20made%20on%20Bitcoin%20blockchain%20in%202022

[8] "Covid-19 Boosted the Adoption of Digital Financial Services." World Bank. July 21, 2022. https://www.worldbank.org/en/news/feature/2022/07/21/covid-19-boosted-the-adoption-of-digital-financial-services.

their wealth. Africa, the poorest continent, is also the world's youngest continent, with the highest adoption of cell phones. Bitcoin usage in Africa is exploding. Among many innovations taking hold there is a text transaction service that analog phones can use. This overcomes the need for smartphones which are much less common.

The power to accrue wealth stored safely on your phone, instead of having to protect it physically, is a core aspect of why Bitcoin is so inspiring. Corrupt governments routinely confiscate wealth, and countries where large-scale violence is commonplace, make protecting physical assets a matter of life and death. Refugees fleeing their homes can take their Bitcoin anywhere, across any border.

Because each Bitcoin can be subdivided into 100,000,000 sub-units, it is an ideal tool for accumulating even micro amounts. This makes Bitcoin equally suitable for the ultra-wealthy and those with next to nothing. Bitcoin's divisibility also provides the roadmap for how ongoing price appreciation in fiat can work. As the price of Bitcoin in fiat rises, the amount of Bitcoin required to buy things priced in fiat simply drops. The more one Bitcoin is worth, the few sub-units are required to buy real-world items. This is already happening all over the world. The price of an average home in British Columbia in 2016 was 600BTC that number today is roughly 40BTC.

Divisibility is also a key defense mechanism to protect Bitcoin against government or institutional capture. The more money spent to buy it will only result in smaller and smaller units being used functionally as the overall price goes up. At some point continuing to buy will require more and more paper fiat money. Creating that money will weaken that money simultaneously making bitcoin harder and more valuable.

Turkey has just eclipsed 85% of inflation. Banks in Lebanon are freezing assets. This year, there have been several bank robberies in Lebanon where people are just trying to withdraw their own money.[9] The ability to safely custody your wealth is a significant advance in technology. However, it's not on the radar of many people living in first-world countries.

It will not be the 40 million Canadians that move the price of Bitcoin significantly. It may not even be the Western world. It will be the billions of people living in countries without access to financial services and those living under crippling inflation due to gross mismanagement of their local fiat currency.

Even if the innovation described is not hitting your wow factor, please understand that there are well over 1 billion people for whom it could be life-changing. If you think it terms of the potential growth of network traffic, having an accessible solution to a foundational quality of life problem for over one billion people is a tremendous potential market for any product, let alone one that already has almost two hundred million users.

Bitcoin the Network

"We see Bitcoin as potentially the greatest social network of all." – Tyler Winklevoss

A great way to address one of the most common starting place objections regarding the intrinsic value of an intangible asset is understanding

---

[9] "Lebanon hit by string of bank robberies as citizens try to claim own savings." Euronews. September 16, 2022. https://www.euronews.com/2022/09/16/lebanon-hit-by-string-of-bank-robberies-as-citizens-try-to-claim-own-savings.

Bitcoin as a network. When talking to advisors about Bitcoin, I often get the idea that they believe it can still go to zero because there is no underlying physical asset. This is not to say that Bitcoin cannot go to zero. I understand that is a possibility, nothing is certain, and no one has a crystal ball. But we do know a lot about networks, how they behave and what growth cycles look like. People who understand hard money and not Bitcoin often like the idea of a gold-backed cryptocurrency. Many struggle to understand how an asset like Bitcoin can be hard when no physical asset exists.

Networks themselves have tremendous value. The internet and smartphones are two great examples. The more the user base grows, the more traffic happens on the network. This increased traffic creates economic opportunity and ingenuity, which results in utility. The more utility, the more users the network attracts. This cycle played out in both previous examples and is playing out in Bitcoin now.

The internet started as email, static web pages, and search engines. Rising internet traffic created new online business opportunities, which birthed online payment providers that added a new utility for web surfers, offering them new products and services they previously did not have access to locally. That, in turn, attracted more users to the internet, and so on.

In the case of Bitcoin, as discussed in the previous section, the network has the potential to create access to wealth creation for over a billion people. There are already well over 100 million people using the network. Regarding networks, 100 million users is a significant milestone in terms of the likelihood of that network hitting a billion users. For the internet to have moved between those two numbers took about eight years. Based on Bitcoin's rate of current network expansion, we are somewhere between three to four years from hitting one billion Bitcoin users. With cell phones and the internet, the path to 50% of the planet accelerates once you have eclipsed a billion users. Bitcoin's route to a billion users is clear, as there is already that number of people without access to conventional banks. The market for this service already exists.

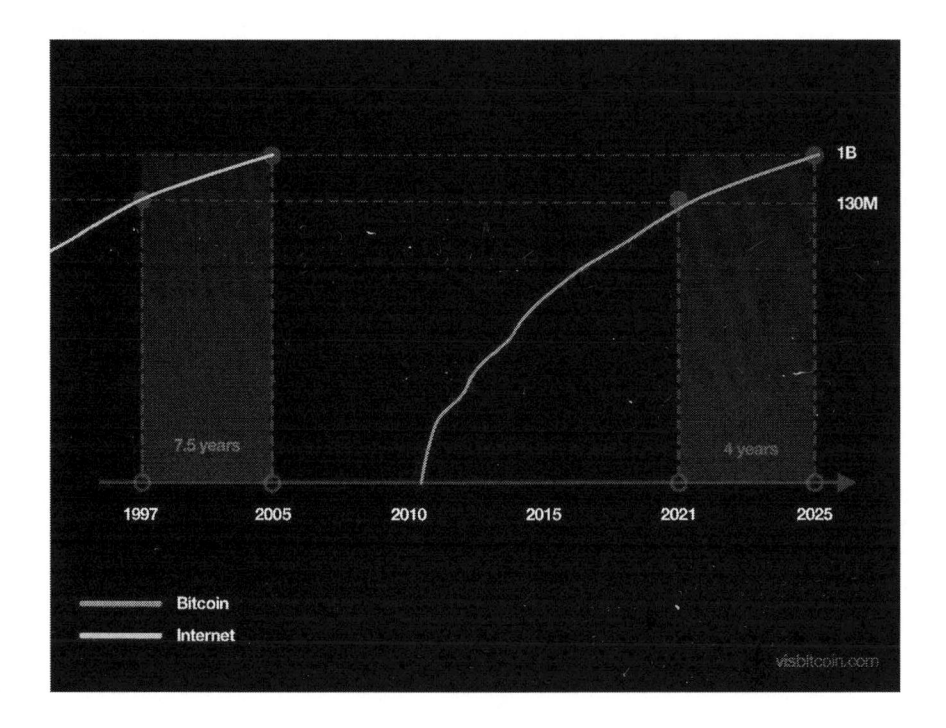

![Chart comparing Bitcoin and Internet adoption. Internet: 1997 to 2005, 7.5 years to 1B users. Bitcoin: 2010 to 2021 at 130M users, projected 4 years to 2025 for 1B. Source: visbitcoin.com]

The Bitcoin network has roughly the same number of users today that the internet had in 1997. For those who were around and using computers at that time, it can be easy to forget exactly how much has changed. I started university in 1998 and, at that time, got my first university email address. Back then, email was still rare enough in my life that I routinely missed messages from my professors because email itself was not yet part of the way life worked for me. Because of my age, I have always worked in a serious job in that email played an important role. I lived through the time when email transitioned from not even knowing why I needed it to not being able to work without it.

The Bitcoin network runs 24/7, which means the market for buying and selling Bitcoin never stops. It's a global asset that moves freely between international borders, with the buyers and sellers not needing to know who the other is. Regarding the potential economy to be built on top of the network, we are only just beginning to scratch the surface.

It has not happened yet, but one day Bitcoin may be an asset held by and traded between Countries. The transparency of Bitcoin holdings makes it an ideal asset for international exchange, particularly between countries with low trust. Richard Nixon suspended gold redemptions in 1971, calling into question how much gold the Federal Reserve actually had. This problem would be simple to solve using Bitcoin. Additionally, the recent events of freezing US treasuries held by Russia have already created the case for countries holding uncensorable assets. Nations are unlikely to want to keep assets that other governments could freeze. Bitcoin is an asset that cannot be frozen and could add a new dimension to geopolitics.

The potential market for Bitcoin users ranges from a farmer in Nigeria to the Bank of China. Bitcoin itself is something that could one-day birth new financial services products. Businesses and technologies that have not yet been dreamed of will be built on the Bitcoin network. It will enable new ways of commerce not yet imagined. When you have a currency that can be exchanged B2B internationally without counterparty risk, you have a tool to unlock entirely new ways of doing business. Look at the advancements that the internet created in online payments. Companies like PayPal solved a need caused by the invention of the internet and, as a result, started entirely new economies built online. Bitcoin will take that evolution one step further by providing a global and borderless currency, that settles finally, and excludes no one.

The Bitcoin network can also be thought of as a base layer for value transfer for which further layers can be built on top. In the 1990s the base layer internet TCP-IP did not have the data throughput to allow for 4k video streaming on handheld devices. Similarly the infrastructure and tools to allow that kind functionality such as fibre-optic cables, smart phones, and high-speed modems also did not exist. These were subsequent innovations, built on top of the base layer ecosystem provided by the world wide web. The bitcoin network also has this promise and in understanding or assessing Bitcoin as a network it's a healthy comparison to keep in mind how early we are in terms of the overall evolution of the ecosystem. In this regard it is much like the early internet. The hard monetary rules of the bitcoin protocol do not change, but the Bitcoin community globally is very busy building and imagining all kinds of functionality on top of the base network that today does not exist. The most high-profile example of this is the lightning network, which is a relay system that allows for the exchange of Bitcoins to happen without every single transaction being posted individually to the base network (creating an impossible bottleneck based on growing traffic volume). Lightning as an innovation could transform the base layer of Bitcoin into a functional global payments network in time. There are layers even being dreamt of on-top of lightning already, this is a discussion for a different book.

Bitcoin The Element

"Bitcoin is a technological tour de force." – Bill Gates

Bitcoin is the currency of the Bitcoin network. We tend to think of currency as paper, but in the past, currency was coins made of precious metals. Bitcoin has properties that make its currency rare and precious.

By extension, its currency should be thought of as having more in common with gold coins than today's paper money. Is Bitcoin an element? A natural resource? I believe it is something like this. Perhaps somewhere in the middle. The logic is this; you have something that is precious, scarce, and has been created through a labor-intensive process. That process is proof of work consensus –the brute force computation done by the Bitcoin miners running the network. The product is physically intangible but has many of the characteristics of gold – with a significant difference, gold the element is very heavy. This feature of gold makes storing and transferring in large quantities problematic. However, Bitcoin, the element, is weightless, which would, by weight, make it the first element on the Periodic Table.[10] This feature means that Bitcoin, the element, can be moved anywhere in the world that has electricity and the internet within minutes.

We've never really had the opportunity to invest in something on a broad scale where the total amount available is known and verifiable. There will only ever be 21 million Bitcoin. On top of that, many of those bitcoins, possibly 5 million or more, have been lost forever, making bitcoin already much scarcer than most realize. Bitcoin cannot be confiscated. Suppose access to a bitcoin wallet is lost, or someone dies while their bitcoin keys are with them. In that case, those bitcoins are permanently out of circulation. The number of bitcoins out of circulation will grow over time, which means that Bitcoin has become the only verifiably scarce asset. And it's already scarcer than most people realize. Unlike gold Bitcoin, the intangible and precious resource, cannot be harvested from the dead.

---

[10] Svanholm, Knut. Everything Divided by 21,000,000. Self-published, 2022.

The rate of new bitcoin released into the network is also designed to reduce by 50% every four years. This event is called 'halving.' The halving means from an investment standpoint that Bitcoin is unique in that its stock-to-flow ratio – the measurement of how many years it would take for the existing amount of something to be created again based on the current rate of production – doubles every four years by design. We have never had the opportunity to invest in something that essentially becomes from a production standpoint, exponentially scarcer over time. The gold stock-to-flow ratio is 62. Sixty-two years to produce the amount of gold that currently exists again, based on how much is presently mined per year. Today Bitcoin is 56 – but after the next halving in 2024, that number will double to 112. By 2028 it will be 224. You can see where this is going.

Halving's create built-in and reliably reoccurring supply shocks. Again, try to imagine a world where nation-states are significant holders of Bitcoin. What will these four-year cycles mean to price in another 20 or 40 years?

New Bitcoins will be mined until around 2140. At that time, we will have over 120 years of history. The network can undoubtedly be enduring and permanent and those building bitcoin tools today are planning on it. How will the market price an asset with exponentially growing users and exponentially shrinking production?

Some hold the opinion that Bitcoin is better described as digital property, even more than as money or currency. Again, it is an asset that cannot be confiscated, where owners can prove ownership absolutely, so it certainly has the characteristics of property even though it is physically intangible. If you view it as such, then Bitcoin also becomes simultaneously the scarcest and most universally accessible type of property available. Meaning it should then also be the most appealing property available to anyone. Real estate markets have several barriers of entry, multiple ongoing costs including taxes and upkeep, and are much less liquid. Ownership of keys to a bitcoin wallet does confer the benefits of owning the bitcoin in that wallet- no different than a deed to a piece of land. It could be all of these things. Bitcoin is continually evolving and today people have several ideas about what it is or might be.

In Canada, Bitcoin is considered a commodity. This provides another reason why Bitcoin is considered by many to have been discovered like an element instead of invented. This also explains why Bitcoin is different from every other subsequent cryptocurrency. The distinction is that it will never again be possible to create such a robust network and have the founders remain anonymous/pseudo-anonymous. The person or persons credited with the white paper that became the Bitcoin project went by the pseudonym, Satoshi Nakamoto. That person has never identified themselves publicly. As proof, there is a Bitcoin wallet known to be linked to them, which has never been touched.

Satoshi's anonymity is an essential feature of Bitcoins origin. It makes bitcoin the money that can be considered closest to the goal of not having a corruptible person be in charge of creating that money. Since no person in history has ethically wielded that power over time, this person accomplished the closest possible version of abdicating that power as early as possible. In doing so, they also removed a point of failure. Satoshi's real identity would undoubtedly be a disappointment to the world, whoever they are. No person is perfect, and that person coming forward would be immediately under intense scrutiny, not to mention likely putting their life in danger. The funds inside Satoshi's wallet, some one million BTC, cannot move if that person intends to remain anonymous. The funds would be traceable to whatever bank ultimately cashed the BTC into fiat.

Let's put all this aside. Say it was possible to launch a large traction currency anonymously at any point in the future, even one with principles superior to Bitcoin. No one would want to do it. Bitcoin 2.0 would discredit both bitcoin and itself. The reason for the latter is that this invention would imply the possibility of it happening an endless number of times again. Thus, the birth of Bitcoin is a one-time event. This is why Bitcoin can be said to have unique characteristics from any other cryptocurrency existing now or ever.

I often get questions about regulation and whether or not Bitcoin is a security. Bitcoin cannot be a security for several reasons. Most importantly (firstly), Bitcoin is not a business; there is no Bitcoin-the-company, with a profit motive or board of directors dictating its advertising or strategy. And secondly, no one has successfully stepped forward to claim credit for its creation personally. So, there is no one head of the snake to cut off or identify as the person or persons who benefit from creating it. Bitcoin is an open-source software that anyone can download and participate in. While the expectation of appreciation is important in attracting new users, no entity promises appreciation as a strategy to attract customers. Bitcoin cannot be a security any more than email can, they are both open-source software for exchanging information.

This is why Bitcoin has the properties of a precious natural resource, even if it is man-made and exists only in cyberspace.

Absolute Scarcity

"When someone tries to buy all the world's supply of a scarce asset, the more they buy the higher the price goes. At some point, it gets too expensive for them to buy any more." – Satoshi Nakamoto

The case for not talking to clients about Bitcoin is easy. Governments are going to try and make it illegal. It's too risky. Too volatile. As an advisor responsible for managing other people's money, what you do not want to do is lose their money.

Let's consider the reverse scenario. What if Bitcoin isn't any of those things, but it is just too early to know during this short time it has existed? Imagine it is April 2026, and Bitcoin has just smashed through USD250,000 and eclipsed 1 billion users. Your top 5 clients ask you why they have no exposure; at that point, you still do not fully understand what Bitcoin is. How is that conversation going to go?

This example is not so much about whatever price Bitcoin may eventually hit. I recently posed a similar question to a pension fund manager who told me Bitcoin was too volatile to ever be in pensions. I asked him, "How long can you ignore the best-performing asset before you can be considered negligent in your duties?" He laughed at me.

No one knows what the future holds, and I am trying to avoid wild proclamations. The point of this book is to encourage further education, not advocate for specific strategies today or cast proclamations. It is also true to say that no one knows Bitcoins theoretical maximum price. Any attempts to theorize where Bitcoin will settle in terms of size as an asset class, are educated guesses at best.

One potential scenario worth discussing is called 'Hyperbitcoinization,' which can be described as the most bullish scenario for Bitcoin as a monetary network. Hyperbitcoinization is an idea most people have a hard time accommodating when they hear about it for the first time. From the standpoint of a risk manager, this is the one scenario where a Bitcoin bear does not want to end up being wrong. I debated included this topic at all, as it firmly falls into the category of if you explain it wrong it sounds insane- but I think it's important to touch on as it really conveys the disparity of on one end – you have people who don't understand Bitcoin and think it might be a passing fad, and on the other hand you have people studying Bitcoin constantly who believe it has a much different destiny.

Hyperbitcoinization is the term that refers to an outcome where Bitcoin has successfully demonetized every other form of money in the world. This is the endpoint of the game theory model mentioned in a previous section. Eventually, the incentive for cooperation in using Bitcoin, gains critical mass and is too rewarding to ignore for all levels of participants – individuals, businesses, governments, etc. Today it is one of many potential outcomes, but it has a non-zero chance of happening. Brilliant people have examined this idea in detail and deem it sound.

The more I learn about Bitcoin, the more I think the odds of hyperbitcoinization happening are pretty likely. I also believe that it will happen much sooner than most people think. I want to qualify that statement before moving on by first saying that "sooner than most think" could very well mean another 25 years or more. If you look at how the internet continues to evolve 25 years after hitting 100 million users, it is still maturing as a tool, and growing in terms of its societal influence. The internet's transition to mass adoption happened in a relatively short time frame, but it remains a work in progress, and is only becoming more entrenched in daily life as time passes. We have not yet arrived at a final version of the internet. We are nowhere near a final version of Bitcoin. Bitcoin provides a superior solution for a good (money) that everyone in the world needs to survive. It exists in a world where its competition has had no incentive to improve over time. The current market of money users are captive hostages. A transition to a Bitcoin based global economy might seem fast in hindsight but I suspect in real time will still feel so slow that it will seem unlikely until the process has almost entirely unfolded.

Hyperbitcoinization could occur simply as a result of Bitcoin continuing to grow organically and not breaking. It is already a better form of money than what is used day to day. As Bitcoin grows in users and mass, we are approaching a moment where a threshold percent of the human population (whatever that number is) will realize that the price of Bitcoin will eventually go up endlessly if you endlessly print more money. At that moment, there will be a stampede to get whatever money you have out of the monopoly money that can be created because governments say so and into the finite, hard money. This idea is already well underway today. I can guarantee you that. I can say this confidently because many people worldwide who have chosen to store monetary energy in Bitcoin have simply realized the possibility of this event before everyone else. Many others will have this same revelation I and millions of others have had, and when they do, they too will be compelled to tell others. That is why Bitcoin is exciting and inspiring. When you understand it, you want to help others understand it too. People will do that because they already are. As more people spread the idea, the idea will spread faster. Hope is contagious, and when you understand the hope Bitcoin offers of a fairer financial future, you will also want to tell your clients.

Bitcoin is a currency that essentially works opposite to every other currency. The idea is that central banks continually printing money will over time only increase the value inherent in bitcoin's enforceable scarcity. As money expands, the gap between the value of ever-expanding money and verifiably scarce money will become more and more dramatic. Essentially, Bitcoin invalidates inflationary monetary policy as a viable long-term strategy.

Bitcoin is the first and only time we will see Gresham's law play out digitally. Gresham's law is an economic principle that says overvalued currency will tend to drive undervalued currency out of circulation. This phenomena has been observed in history many times both in the ancient world and medieval times where the quality of metal coins in circulation was not uniform. Coins with similar face value, but different real value leads to the more intrinsically valuable coins being hoarded, while the coins with less intrinsic value are spent and circulate more freely. This in turn makes the good money even more valuable, relative to the lower quality coins.

Gresham's law plays out to completion as more and more market participants understand the value gap between different currencies. The free market will eventually self-select the money with superior qualities, driving the value out of the inferior money. As this relates to Bitcoin and hyperbitcoinization, a tiny percent of the worlds population understands this today, and they are already hoarding it out of circulation. Of the nineteen million bitcoin circulating today, less than 2 million are listed on exchanges and 70% have not moved in over a year.

We have seen many currencies collapse throughout history over and over again. It's not as though we do not understand how this process unfolds. Fiat money works when there is an implied confidence that the paper is worth what the government says it is worth. But it's just paper and a promise. That promise has been broken every time human beings have been trusted to protect the value of money. So, as currencies all over the world expand and lose value relative to Bitcoin – the hyperbitcoinization theory suggests that one by one, starting with the weakest, currencies will succumb. The open market will select the superior money. As that happens, it is theorized that once the process is triggered, it will only accelerate.

The core of the prisoner's dilemma is trust among players. Regarding Central Banks, the question is whether they can sincerely expect to trust each other- as economic principles already proven to fail over time, begin their inevitable crumble. Will they not cave in and adopt Bitcoin even as an asset to back their local currency as their inflated currencies struggle to retain value?

Today, only El Salvador is openly accumulating Bitcoin as a nation-state. In theory, every central bank country can still print whatever money they require to start buying Bitcoin – hard money that is finite. The fraternity of central banks has so far held firm. The IMF has served as both the carrot and the stick dissuading further countries beyond El Salvador defecting from fiat[11]. Civil unrest due to the rising cost of living is spreading worldwide, and desperation creates unpredictable behavior. We are already seeing a rejection of the unipolar world order, and the BRICS countries are talking about creating a new currency, potentially backed by commodities that could challenge or supplant

---

[11] "US Stocks and Bonds Rally After Weak Jobs Data." Financial Times, 4 Sept. 2021, www.ft.com/content/c36c45d2-1100-4756-a752-07a217b2bde0.

the US dollar as a global reserve.[12] The endless expansion of the US dollar alone is exporting inflation globally. It is not hard to imagine a scenario where local politics force world leaders to consider alternatives out of self-preservation. Eventually, we could even see a truly desperate regime decide to destroy its currency to create enough money to buy a meaningful amount of Bitcoin.

Fiat currencies rely on a combination of trust and force. Both can be stress tested if the currency cannot perform its basic duties. When a currency loses value and confidence, and those countries are backed into a corner by extreme inflation, instability creates unpredictable outcomes. This is how coups and revolutions happen. Again, we haven't seen many of these happen where Bitcoin as a viable alternative money already existed. When Venezuela's currency collapsed and hyperinflated in 2016, Bitcoin was far too young to be a serious solution. Over time Bitcoin could become a tempting option for countries to convert to another currency with firm rules and value based on scarcity as a tool for political change or political survival.

Game theory playing out in real time applies to individuals trying to do what they think is best for their families. It also applies to the politicians running countries. This game theory at the individual level has been playing out now for over 13 years. Many people worldwide have chosen Bitcoin as their preferred safe haven for monetary value. That number is also one that will grow as more users come, and more people understand the value proposition fully.

---

[12] Chernenko, Demid. "Can BRICS dedollarize the global financial system?" Cambridge University Press, 2020. https://www.cambridge.org/core/elements/can-brics-dedollarize-the-global-financial-system/0AEF98D2F232072409E9556620AE09B0.

If that all sounds crazy, there is already not enough Bitcoin in the world for every millionaire to have just one. The Bitcoin game theory can play out on multiple levels within countries, provinces, cities, and between corporations and individuals. Bitcoin is much scarcer and harder than almost everyone realizes. It is a potential life raft for whoever wants to hop in. Hyperbitcoinization is when all the ships start to sink at once, and there is only one life raft. Mass adoption could very well mean the end of the dilutive fiat currency model. In that outcome Bitcoin, the high performing investment, is a Trojan Horse for Bitcoin, the global hard money.

The other important thing to keep in mind is that there is also no known endpoint to currency dilution. Theoretically, you can lose half of the value of your money an infinite number of times so long as the mandate to use that money remains intact. In this respect, Bitcoin is not just different from existing government monies; it is their antithesis.

We have never seen an experiment like this in human history because it was technologically impossible before the discovery of Bitcoin. Thanks to the 14 years of QE since the 2008 crisis, we also have unprecedented debt levels in the system. Debt will make avoiding ongoing money printing very difficult.

So when is the right time to start learning about Bitcoin? At what point did the internet become impossible to ignore? In the early internet days, businesses did not need a webpage. Later they did not have an online strategy. Today you need multiple strategies for every different social media platform.

Once a technology that represents an improvement to the previous way of doing things takes hold, it typically becomes more ingrained in society. Continuous evolution happens until it is replaced by something else. The current adoption rate of Bitcoin makes one wonder how other monetary networks will survive and thrive in a world where one network offers users significantly more favorable terms than all other alternatives. Whether or not hyperbitcoinization occurs, its likelihood to continue to attract users and other nation-states is promising. Bitcoins permanently fixed supply means that as a prospective investment – these are all indicators that Bitcoins future price appreciation still has much upside.

Don't Be Charlie Munger

"Bitcoin is stupid, evil, and makes me look bad." – Charlie Munger

Bitcoin is an underappreciated evolution in accounting, which allows for an entirely new way to transact value without an intermediary anywhere in the world. It was engineered to offer a superior alternative to every other monetary network in the world and is still in its infancy. It is designed to be the hardest currency on the planet and the scarcest resource. It is growing on an adoption curve more viral than the internet. It allows billions of users in poverty to accumulate wealth in a meaningful way for the first time ever and has already achieved a massive user base including one sovereign nation. Layers are being built on top of it with the assumption that it will endure for decades. And due to its permanently fixed supply, any portion you can secure as a percentage of the total available will never change. This is not simply a speculative tech play with extreme volatility and a high chance of ceasing to exist. It is a battle-tested, global network attracting innovative minds from every corner of the world. If you are still not sold on the idea of Bitcoin, or Bitcoin for your clients' portfolios- hopefully at least you are starting to understand the need for an informed opinion as to why. The likelihood that Bitcoin will at some point reach a new all-time in price is at least as likely that it will simply go away. As I stated at the outset, I always approach financial advisors from the position of understanding that the broad majority of advisors primary aspiration is to help their clients. That can mean a lot of different things, but above all it means being informed. In the case of Bitcoin it means being prepared for the outcome where Bitcoin outperforms. My experience learning about Bitcoin is that the people with the most conviction about it are the ones who understand it the best. It is for this reason that I believe so strongly that if average investors truly knew how to evaluate Bitcoin, they would be more comfortable making an allocation to it.

Now to pose a different question worth considering. Suppose we were to describe this type of technology to an expert investor and ask their opinion on whether or not to hold some of it. Would we ask the 90-year-old guru or a 50-year-old who has grown up in the internet age instead? I ask this question because many legendary investors, including Munger and Warren Buffet, have been notoriously bearish on Bitcoin. Charlie Munger often refers to it as rat poison. These opinions are usually based on the same complaints, such as no underlying asset supporting it, which merely demonstrates a lack of a basic understanding of everything Bitcoin represents.

In April 2022, when the price was USD43,000, Peter Thiel, the founder of PayPal, was quoted as saying he thought Bitcoin could easily increase in price another 100x, to well over USD4,000,000. This is not about price predictions. I am highlighting the need to consider where you are going because of your opinions on Bitcoin. Many very wealthy, highly successful investors are holding and advocating for Bitcoin.

This is a critical point to understand for advisors and their clients. Most high-profile people commenting publicly on Bitcoin would be incapable of writing this book today. I have no problem taking the advice of the most successful investors in history. Still, I wouldn't put much value into their assessment of technology this revolutionary. Such an assessment requires a considerable investment of time to understand. Also, it could potentially be detrimental to the system which made those very gurus rich in the first place.

Another challenge is if you look around for other ideas about where Bitcoin might go from a planning perspective – there isn't a ton. I fully understand that advisors' inherent fiduciary responsibilities include properly assessing and managing risk. This is why you don't see advisors publicly espousing cutting-edge ideas about Bitcoin in portfolios en masse. Dealers and Regulators play a key role as well. I have met a handful of advisors who understand Bitcoin. Yet, typically they express fear in talking about it because they do not want to jeopardize their business or licenses.

This is how we arrived at this point. There is an asset that has just had the best ten-year returns in history, and is almost 70% off its all-time high, with favorable conditions to continue to outperform. Yet there are practically no advisors avidly recommending their clients look at it.

Addressing Common Concerns

"My very humble assessment is that it is worth nothing," – ECB President Christine Lagarde

Advisors hoping for credible conversations with clients regarding Bitcoin should understand clients' questions or reservations in making an informed decision. Here I will attempt to address a handful of the most common Bitcoin misconceptions from a Bitcoiner's perspective.

Bitcoin Sentiment

Bitcoin Sentiment is the most apparent objection Advisors likely will encounter if ever talking to clients about Bitcoin. Imagine those already fearful of losses and ill-equipped to ride market volatility now debating a position in the most volatile asset class. Bitcoin price narratives are just as strong as the price action itself. When things are good, everyone wants it. When things are bad, everyone believes this is finally the time that Bitcoin will collapse entirely and go to zero.

Patient, long-term planners have a high chance of being rewarded with Bitcoin positions. Especially those who have the emotional fortitude to consider buying during times of extremely negative sentiment. A solid understanding of Bitcoin will help people make an investment decision based on fundamentals – such as the growth of the network and the amount of money being moved on it. The same people could be guided to ignore what is said on tv.

Even though Bitcoin has held very high prices for several years now, there is some underlying expectation that it will still fail and vanish. While not impossible, that outcome for Bitcoin would contradict what we know about networks and adoption. One way to put this anxiety to rest is to look at the times in history when other transformative technologies were also viewed as fads. Radio, the internet, and even automobiles all had their detractors at some point.

The Bitcoin Experiment Has Failed

Regardless of what you do upon finishing this book, please avoid this opinion at all costs. Bitcoin has already proven to be incredibly durable and collapse resistant. The smaller it is as an asset, the less money is required to move the price up or down. As it remains small in the grand scheme of global asset classes, we can continue to expect the bull-bear cycles in Bitcoin to have a lot of volatility.

Bitcoin is an intangible asset, with no country or bank behind it, that recently crashed to 'only' USD20,000. This is the validation for some that the idea has failed. Think about that for a second. Bitcoin will fail only when its encryption is broken, or a malicious actor gains control of 51% of the network and sabotages it. Any other scenario, particularly as it relates merely to measuring the price in a fiat currency, is useless to judge Bitcoin's likelihood of long-term survival. The opinion that the jury is out is fair. However, say anyone proclaims they now have proof that Bitcoin has failed. In that instance, they ignore the simple reality of what Bitcoin has already achieved and continues to accomplish every day it exists.

Bitcoin is a Ponzi

A Ponzi scheme is a form of fraud. It lures investors with the promise of outsized returns. It creates the illusion of those returns by paying profits to earlier investors with funds from more recent investors. The argument that Bitcoin is a Ponzi makes sense to many outsiders. Those who understood Bitcoin and invested early have seen the value of their Bitcoins appreciate astronomically as the result of more people joining the network after they did.

Ponzis are an organized mechanism. They use the new money entering into the scheme to pay those already in. Hence it creates the false appearance of profit that doesn't exist, built on top of a never-ending pyramid that must grow forever to satisfy the profit chain. Bitcoin does not generate a yield of any kind. Existing holders of Bitcoins receive no ongoing dividends or interest, and there is no guarantee that the price will go up.

There is also no one at the top of Bitcoin recruiting new victims to the scheme. While there are several high-profile Bitcoiners, no one speaks on behalf of Bitcoin, and the Bitcoin community has made that clear many times.

One such example of this played out recently as Craig S. Wright came forward claiming that he was the anonymous founder of Bitcoin, Satoshi Nakamoto. Wright's claim, along with his inability to produce sufficient evidence to back it up, has largely been met with disdain within the Bitcoin community. After filing a defamation lawsuit against a Bitcoiner known on Twitter as Hodlnaut over tweets denying his claims, Wright was countersued and lost in Norwegian court, to the bitcoin communities chagrin.[13] Anyone attempting again to reveal themselves as Satoshi without ironclad proof now risks their personal credibility as well as taking on a financial/legal risk. The Bitcoin community has not taken Wright's claims lightly. Any person considering this in the future can expect a similar response mustered, so unless someone can prove access to Satoshi's wallet, I can't imagine this happening again.

Bitcoin is a faceless, decentralized protocol anyone can download and participate in. The value of more people joining the Bitcoin network is that the percentage of Bitcoin anyone currently owns as a total percentage of the Bitcoin network can never change. New users are attracted based on the opportunity to participate in global currency, free from centralized institutions which cannot be arbitrarily diluted. Bitcoins value proposition attracts lasting users, and as a result, the price

---

[13] Ligon, Cheyenne. "Crypto Twitter Took Center Stage During the First Day of Hodlonaut Vs. Craig Wright." CoinDesk. September 12, 2022. https://www.coindesk.com/business/2022/09/12/crypto-twitter-took-center-stage-during-the-first-day-of-hodlonaut-vs-craig-wright/.

can appreciate. As more and more people grasp Bitcoin, more long-term holders are born. As more and more supply of Bitcoin is removed from the market, the power of its transparent scarcity will become more and more obvious.

The Greater Fool Theory

The Greater Fool Theory is a variation of the Ponzi argument. It assumes Bitcoin has value only so long as there is someone out there dumber than you who will be willing to buy it from you at a higher price than you paid for it. The greater fool theory is another way to summarize the aforementioned Peter Schiff, who believes that Bitcoin has no intrinsic value. It is also an idea to which many who have incredibly high trust in the system, which I mentioned in the foreword, adhere.

The Bitcoin network offers enforceable scarcity via transparent digital records of accounts. This technology, and what it enables, is the value. Those willing to buy and hold Bitcoin for the long term understand this premise. They participate based on the assumption that this innovation will become increasingly crucial as fiat currencies become increasingly abundant. It's not a matter of who is the greater fool. Proponents of Bitcoin have likely arrived at this point through hours of research, typically on the history of fiat money, Austrian economics, and hard assets. The community has concluded that most, if not all, of the world's economic problems (and many non-economic), are rooted in unsound currency. It takes hours of study to understand this argument for Bitcoin fully. The argument may yet prove incorrect. But foolish is probably not the right word to describe an idea that many of the world's most innovative, wealthiest minds have vetted after intense study and taken on board.

The Price Cannot Go Up Forever

There is a strong urge to believe that because Bitcoin has already attained a remarkable appreciation in price, it cannot continue to outperform every other asset. Call this the 'what goes up must come down' theory. This narrative returns every time Bitcoin has hit a cycle top price. The report also brings forth the common refrain that finally, this time is the time when Bitcoin has hit its forever all-time price. Whatever the cause for a significant drawdown in Bitcoin price, without fail, is when bears come forward to proclaim that Bitcoin has finally failed.

Bitcoin is the only asset you can buy with a theoretical price maximum of infinity. Even the Simpsons (known for their ability to predict the future) have joked that one day, Bitcoin's price will be ∞.[14] If the hyperbitcoinization theory proves correct, Bitcoin will reach equilibrium when it has swallowed every other inferior fiat currency globally. But hyperbitcoinization does not need to occur for Bitcoin to keep growing in price well beyond its previous all-time highs.

There is skepticism that Bitcoin will do what it has always done and resume rising again at some point. This often is related to an opinion that astronomical price targets for Bitcoin must be based on pure fantasy. This is also not the case. Many mathematical models support long-term sustained appreciation of Bitcoin's price that does not depend on all other monies collapsing. I will highlight one of my personal favorites – the Greg Foss model. Greg is one of the most successful high

---

[14] "Simpsons episode made bitcoin prediction and referenced infinity, GameStop, and Tesla stock fluctuations." Business Insider. April 14, 2021. https://markets.businessinsider.com/currencies/news/simpsons-episode-bitcoin-prediction-infinity-gamestop-tesla-stock-fluctuate-2021-4-1030297740.

yield credit traders and portfolio managers in Canadian history and someone I strongly recommend as a resource for further learning. He views Bitcoin as insurance against what he calls the fiat Ponzi. His price target is USD 2 million per Bitcoin in today's dollars, not forwardly adjusted.

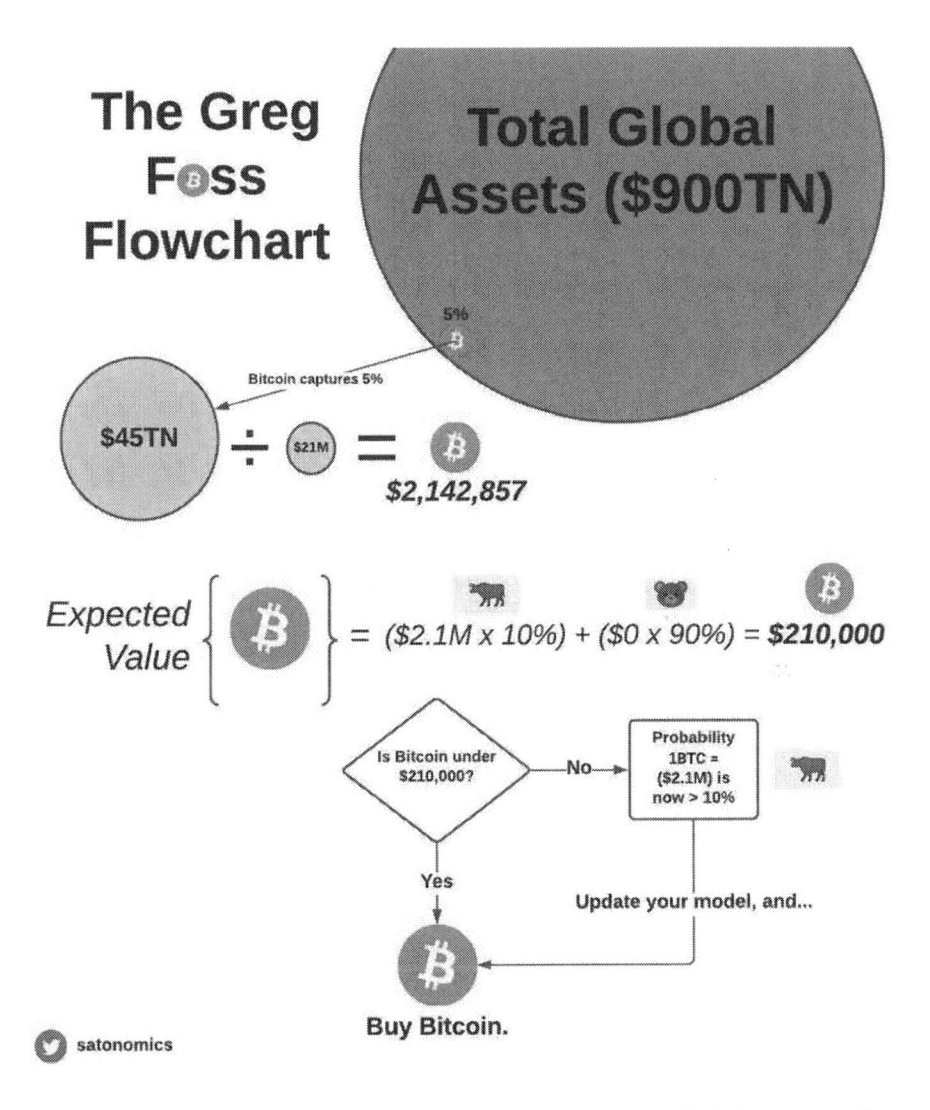

The Greg Foss Flowchart

Total Global Assets ($900TN)

Bitcoin captures 5%

$45TN ÷ $21M = ₿
$2,142,857

Expected Value {₿} = ($2.1M x 10%) + ($0 x 90%) = **$210,000**

Is Bitcoin under $210,000? —No→ Probability 1BTC = ($2.1M) is now > 10%

Yes ↓

Update your model, and...

Buy Bitcoin.

satonomics

The model speculates that Bitcoin capturing 5% of global assets today, creates a market cap of 45T USD, which works out to USD 2.1M per

Bitcoin. Because the supply is permanently capped, there is a straight line between market cap and unit price with Bitcoin that will never change. From an investor standpoint, if you assign a 10% chance of that price happening, you should be willing to pay USD 210,000 for one Bitcoin. At a Bitcoin price of USD 21,000 you are effectively getting 1% odds of this happening.

Greg is just looking at the size of the global asset market and the spiraling debt problem. He then makes a risk-adjusted bet that smart money managers will eventually see Bitcoin as a hedge against inflation that is required to make the math work and prevent a total system collapse. All this example is meant to provide is a different framework for the ongoing increase in value capture by the Bitcoin network. You are entitled to doubt Bitcoin will achieve 5% of the global asset market cap. But remember, many intelligent, successful people view much more bullish scenarios than this one as likely. I am just trying to expose some Bitcoin models to help you form an opinion. Based simply on a USD 300B market cap, Bitcoin has so much opportunity to appreciate in market cap from institutional money alone – broader retail adoption is probably not even required for a six-figure price.

Let's look at Bitcoin's room to appreciate from another perspective. Should it only attain 1% of the 900T available to be invested globally today, that would be a 9T Bitcoin market cap. This would produce a price of USD 430,000 in today's dollars. That's more than a 21x return from a price of USD 20,000. Keep in mind that as inflation continues, the 900T available will also grow. The purchasing power of fiat will continue to diminish as the system continues to expand. However, it also means that higher Bitcoin prices need really only two things – the existing system to continue diluting and Bitcoin not to break.

Bitcoin is Right-Wing / Libertarian / Terrorist Financing / Black Market Money

Attaching Bitcoin to a political opponent has been a popular vector of attack to polarize public sentiment since the time Bitcoin transitioned from concept to working product. The reality is that Bitcoin is apolitical. Bitcoin stands to upset the status quo for all political parties should it successfully disrupt the current financial order on a large scale.

Because Bitcoin is peer-to-peer and cannot be confiscated when cold stored, its existence creates new wrinkles in enforcing traditional financial penalties. The IRS has various bounties for hackers who can provide solutions to cracking aspects of encryption in digital currencies, including how to confiscate cold-stored Bitcoin. These features have, at different times, made Bitcoin and other privacy-based cryptocurrencies ideal for illegal/quasi-legal activity. The now infamous online black-market website known as Silk Road was an early utilizer of Bitcoin's ability to transact pseudo-anonymously across borders. That business gave many the early opinion that that was Bitcoin's primary use case. More recently (in February 2022), in Canada, Bitcoin wallets were used to fund the trucker convoy that gathered in Ottawa. Donors shifted to Bitcoin after the government worked with online provider GoFundMe to shut down traditional public funding of that movement.[15] The political left in Canada painted Bitcoin as a currency used for insurrection.

---

[15] Phillips Erb, Kelly. "IRS Will Pay Up To $625,000 If You Can Crack Monero, Other Privacy Coins." Forbes. September 14, 2020. https://www.forbes.com/sites/kellyphillipserb/2020/09/14/irs-will-pay-up-to-625000-if-you-can-crack-monero-other-privacy-coins/?sh=2b0fd57785cc.

Bitcoin is a tool. How it is used, is up to the user – the same way you can use a hammer as a weapon or to build things. Bitcoin has functionality that may attract illicit activity. However, it also has many people genuinely looking to utilize a superior way to store and exchange value. It also should be noted that Bitcoins transparency and traceability do make it a poor tool for money laundering and illegal activity. While Bitcoin wallets may be anonymous, the fiat bank accounts connected to them are not. Bitcoin funds are much more trackable than the average outsider realizes and do not offer anywhere near the anonymity that cash does.

Because Bitcoin represents an improvement in many ways to previous forms of currency from a technological standpoint, users of Bitcoin are choosing a tool that potentially challenges existing governing models. To say that any particular political faction has adopted Bitcoin or that any group speaks on Bitcoin's behalf is incorrect. Bitcoin is now held in pension funds and on the balance sheets of public companies and nation-states. People will always, to the extent possible based on their local laws and regulations, use Bitcoin however they want within the context of what is possible on the network. This will continue to produce a variety of actors, no different than any other cash currency. The US dollar remains the international currency of illicit activity and fraud. It is also the most widely used currency; most users hold and use US dollars for legal purposes.

Bitcoin Undermines Fiat Currencies

In April of 2022, then-Conservative Party leadership candidate Jean Charest accused rival Pierre Poilievre of 'attacking the legitimacy of the Bank of Canada' when he suggested Canadians should consider Bitcoin as a strategy to escape inflation. Many have adopted some version of this opinion, feeling that Bitcoin's potential to disintermediate Governments from the control of money is dangerous.

I discussed in previous sections the government's promise that money is money in a centralized monetary system. This is the foundation of strangers being able to exchange it with each other and not worry about counterparty risk (beyond counterfeit money). Participants sacrifice in exchange for centralized validation – the control over the policy of how that monetary network functions. Fiat currencies survive based on implied trust and a public consensus of that trust. When trust is lost, flight from cash tends to follow, which is how fiat currencies collapse. This process has not been uncommon in the modern era. Recent examples include Venezuela, Nigeria, and Sri Lanka.

The financial risk posed by currency debasement is apolitical. The solution offered by Bitcoin is not designed to destabilize governments. Fiat currency debasement is a betrayal of the promise made by the issuer. As this relates to Bitcoin, it could be argued that without a point of reference existing outside of the fiat system, the detrimental effect of fiat debasement has been challenging to observe. The prolonged existence of Bitcoin and the growth of its network may make the traditional practice of fiat money supply dilution difficult to carry on. Capital finds its way to a place where its value will be safest. Before Bitcoin's existence, moving capital out of native fiat currency likely made it impossible to use for buying and selling. Bitcoins peer to peer nature and absence of counterparty risk offer a genuine alternative. This does not mean that Bitcoin itself does anything to undermine fiat currency. It merely presents choice and free market competition in money. How fiat currencies respond to this will determine their viability without Bitcoin doing anything other than just being Bitcoin.

It is alternative money with a unique value proposition that can never be diluted without consent.

Cryptocurrency Bankruptcies

2022 was an unmitigated disaster for investors in cryptocurrencies and cryptocurrency companies. The Ontario teachers' pension plan and Caisse de dépôt et placement du Québec (CDQP) made significant investments in cryptocurrency service providers that went bankrupt in 2022. Unfortunately, these investments were made under the misguided opinion that investing in these companies was safer than simply investing in bitcoin.

There is an important distinction to be made between investing in startup tech companies operating in regulatory conditions struggling to understand and keep pace with the innovation happening in fintech and the Bitcoin protocol, which has been running continuously now without error for 13 years.

Again, some of this likely concerns the general ignorance surrounding bitcoin's value proposition. Traditional money managers were led to feel that a safer strategy to participate in this sector was to invest in companies rather than the base asset. They felt this because it conceptually was more reminiscent of typical money management.

Bitcoin's currently unavoidable ties to and unfortunate lumping in with the cryptocurrency industry certainly affect the price action and create negative narratives in the news. However, over the long run, investors who purchase and store their bitcoin are unaffected by these events.

For the Bitcoin network to continue providing its ability to bank the unbanked or store monetary energy in a network that does not constantly dilute, it does not require further evolution or proliferation of cryptocurrency services.

These unfortunate blow-ups have harmed many and made investors skeptical. Still, they are not a reason to avoid bitcoin as an investment on its merit. From a financial education standpoint, cryptocurrency industry practices have, for many, perpetuated the previously mentioned concerns. Bitcoin is some kind of Ponzi. Or, if a publicly traded cryptocurrency can go bankrupt overnight, that must mean bitcoin could as well.

Bitcoin, the technology, was discovered. Those who made that discovery walked away from the project shortly after, never to be heard from again. It is a genuinely community-driven project, immune to any individual or entity taking control of it. Bitcoin is not a business. There are no parties incented to take risks on behalf of its users to make it more successful.

Bitcoin has a straightforward and valuable function. It needs only the internet to exist. For this reason, comparing the Bitcoin network to enterprise fintech companies and unregistered securities casinos makes little sense.

Bitcoin is Unregulated

This is a common and misguided refrain from those who look from the outside at various cryptocurrency scams and the aforementioned bankruptcies of cryptocurrency exchanges. Bitcoin, in Canada is as regulated as it's going to get. It has regulatory clarity as a commodity, and in Canada we have single asset spot ETFs that hold only Bitcoin.

Bitcoin is an opensource software, that anyone can participate in. "Regulating" Bitcoin, would likely be as successful as regulating email. Anyone who wants to use it can.

There is also nothing really to clamp down on in terms of pure Bitcoin. If you are buying Bitcoin, there is only one grade of bitcoin unlike gold. There is only BTC. If you are storing it yourself there is no third party involved.

Confusion around how basic aspects of this works is common. The Canadian government indicated they would ask bitcoin wallet providers to freeze certain wallets in the winter of 2022, to which wallet designer nunchuk.io responded publicly- stating publicly that not only was the request impossible, but that it would never be complied with if it was.

Regulation needs to happen with the companies that serve as access points to customers seeking to buy and store Bitcoin and it surely will. We could also see banks place limitations on the amount of Bitcoin Canadians are allowed to buy. This has already happened in the UK.[16] The Canadian government has placed a $10,000 on cryptocurrency "altcoins", but so far has not made a move to include Bitcoin in this list.

This is again based on a false notion that bitcoin itself is a scam, which we have already discussed at length. People looking to buy bitcoin do not need investor protection from the Bitcoin network, only the

---

[16] "Santander UK - Fraud and Security - Cryptocurrency." Santander UK. Accessed March 31, 2023. https://www.santander.co.uk/personal/support/fraud-and-security/cryptocurrency#:~:text=Limit%20on%20cryptocurrency%20payments&text=a%20%C2%A31%2C000%20limit%20per,any%20rolling%2030%2Dday%20period.

companies who operate in the space of retailing and allowing bitcoin gambling in the form of leveraged long and short trading.

If you simply buy bitcoin and store it in your own wallet, there is nothing to regulate.

Future Innovations in Cryptocurrency Will Surpass Bitcoin

Viewing Bitcoin as an invention invites the rational notion that subsequent inventions will take the best parts of Bitcoin and improve on the concept to create something even better. Bitcoin is the rare case where those who created the original concept got the best possible version the first time around. This is counterintuitive to how most technologies work and the reason why so many diehard crypto investors believe their preferred currency to be the next best thing.

The discovery of Bitcoin was a one-time event that will be impossible to replicate for several reasons. This asset requires a total absence of insiders and a decentralized network highly resistant to external attack. Decentralization in practice is achieved by vast numbers of participants worldwide. Any digital currency that launches from today into forever will have an impossible time not being public about who the founders are. Subsequently, it is impossible to imagine such a project attracting the number of participants required to build a network as decentralized as Bitcoin already. Bitcoin will be more so in the future as it continues to grow.

Bitcoin is not perfect; for example, as a payments network, the base layer is slow. It processes much lower volume than centralized competitors like Visa and Mastercard. Transaction speed and volume is a common point of attack for would-be bitcoin competitors.

A handful of today's projects have even taken the Bitcoin code and changed it in ways the developers viewed as improvements. The market has not embraced any of them on a level anywhere near Bitcoin. Litecoin is the following most significant proof of work cryptocurrency. Although Litecoin is faster than Bitcoin and offers more anonymity and fungibility, Bitcoin is roughly 100x larger than Litecoin today.

There is also the genuine question of network effects, and hyperbitcoinization could easily first extend to crypto payment networks. It is worth wondering how multiple monetary networks can exist simultaneously when one is a superior store of value to another or all others. In theory, over time, users will migrate funds to the network, which proves to be the safest haven for the value of that capital. Upstart challengers attempting to unseat Bitcoin in this respect will have a long way to go in running the gauntlet that Bitcoin has already navigated in surviving and growing over these past 13 years. Many still consider Bitcoin a novelty. Yet, it is a miraculous achievement. A community-managed global currency has been operating for over a decade, survived several 80% drawdowns in price, and has, eventually, resumed growing in size.

To address this specific topic, the question is not so much whether other cryptocurrencies will be able to survive in the long run against Bitcoin. We are just assessing the possibility that a newer network will unseat Bitcoin as the dominant crypto asset at some point down the road. While it's hard for people to believe that we can't always invent a better widget, Bitcoin is not likely to be Myspace to some other projects Facebook.

Bitcoin is a Cult

'Bitcoin fixes this' is a common refrain among those who have bought into the concept that sound money solves most of the world's problems. For those who have not studied Bitcoin and cannot see what Bitcoin enthusiasts see, it would be reasonable to think such ideas were lunacy.

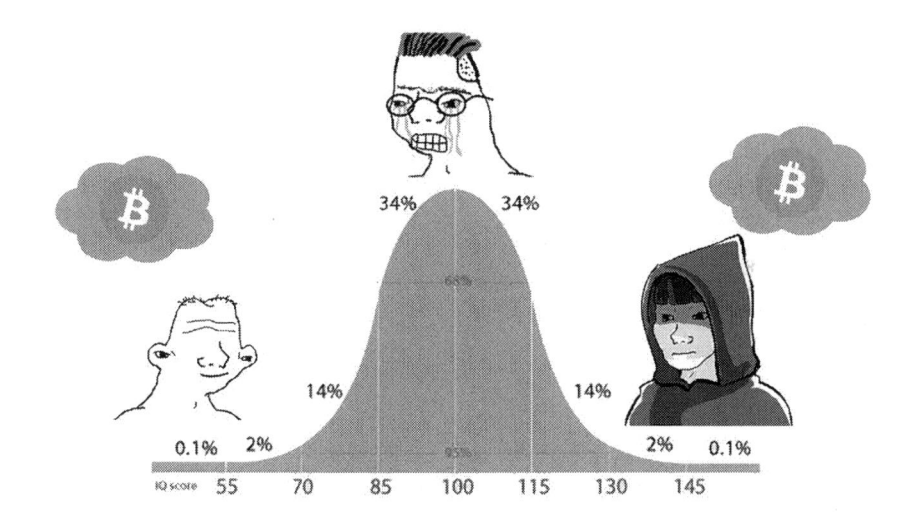

You most certainly do not have to be a genius to understand Bitcoin. Even this can be frustrating for highly educated and intelligent people who have likely not invested the time required to grasp Bitcoin. That group will commonly look at passionate Bitcoin ideas, similarly to how I looked at smartphones when they were first released in the early 2000s- with skepticism and disinterest. Suppose you are not aware you need a new product. In that case, you are unlikely to be excited about whatever new life-changing function that product offers. Most people, even those in financial services, do not adequately understand the disastrous effects of inflationary monetary policy. Keynesian ideas have successfully infiltrated Universities and Government think tanks so long ago that everyone has been raised and educated in this system for generations.

Bitcoin ideas are fascinating. They offer the promise of a financial system rooted in transparency – but those ideas are very foreign to the paradigm society exists in today, where only Governments can issue money. Community enthusiasm, often bordering on zeal, is a feature of bitcoin but should not be confused with making it a cult. It is an idea that inspires hope, and once you see it, it is impossible to unsee.

I urge readers who have held the opinion of Bitcoin being made a cult, to consider the big difference between being a heavily invested fanboy of an idea, and being excited about something that you have studied deeply and understand well. Again, I think a common opinion for those who believe Bitcoin can be culty, is grounded, in just not understanding how much there is to know about the subject of Bitcoin.

Don't Be Frank Giustra

Dear @michael_saylor ,since our debate last April, Bitcoin is down 50%. You call that a store of value? Keep pumping, my friend. Let's touch base after the next big market correction or crisis. Frank Giustra

Frank Giustra is among the world's most successful investors and one of Canada's wealthiest people. He is also the personification of the smart, successful investor who avoids Bitcoin because they don't understand it enough to vet these common criticisms properly. In April 2021, he bravely stepped into a live Bitcoin versus gold debate with one of Bitcoin's most vocal patrons – Michael Saylor.

I can't stress enough how important Michael Saylor's ideas have been in shaping my opinion about Bitcoin, the technology. I strongly recommend readers looking to learn more follow him on Twitter and watch his live interviews.

That Bitcoin vs. gold debate was a resounding victory for Mr. Saylor, but only in the eyes of people who could grasp the nuances of his responses. Giustra, on the other hand, struggled to see how he had lost. Hopefully, at this point, you will appreciate that Bitcoin is much more than a gimmick. It is a complex, and multi-faceted concept that requires a significant time investment to master.

Judging by Mr. Giustra's interviews since the debate, it appears clear he has not yet devoted enough time to understanding Bitcoin to assess it fairly. He has also used this recent price drop as incorrect confirmation that Bitcoin's idea has failed. The moral of this story is to avoid that same trap.

Giustra's other mistake is one that I see often- the opinion that understanding that Bitcoin is internet money equals an understanding of Bitcoin entirely. A great many people who do not own any Bitcoin tell me they understand it. In my time studying Bitcoin, I have yet to meet someone who understood Bitcoin properly and still chose not to own any. Myself, I still regularly learn things about it which are epiphanies for me and even now in writing this book my greatest personal fear is that I am writing it too early in my own journey of learning.

In explaining the concept to others, particularly those with backgrounds in finance I am often reminded of this quote from the Greek philosopher Epictetus- "It is impossible for a man to learn what he thinks he already knows." My advice is to stay humble and curious, and keep in mind we are incredibly early in the Bitcoin process.

Finding a Place for Bitcoin

"If you took a global technology company offering the most desirable product in history and then stripped away all the risks that all companies incur due to their operations and obligations, you would have Bitcoin." Michael Saylor

Hopefully, by now, we have dispelled some misconceptions about Bitcoin. We have clarified the need to consider it on its own merit instead of merely trying to compare it to financial instruments that existed before it.

Bitcoin is not a novelty, and it is unlikely to go away. It is a rapidly growing network offering a service of value to a potential market of billions of users. It is also unlike anything else you might have in your portfolio. It provides both the potential for price appreciation and an inflation hedge. It is something that can be used to buy other things. It has potential as a large-scale collateralizable asset against which to borrow. It is a distinct possibility that it will emerge as the world's dominant monetary network.

The bet on Bitcoin in a portfolio, in my opinion, can also be viewed as insurance on:

a) Fiat monetary system continues onwards, inflating indefinitely (appreciation)
b) Fiat monetary system collapses under the immense pressure of debasement (preservation)

Both scenarios over a long enough time frame are bullish for bitcoin. Suppose the global money supply continues to expand indefinitely. In that case, the finite amount of Bitcoin available will likely appreciate indefinitely. Suppose further the market decides that money based only on debt and credit is worthless when that debt can never be honored. In that case, hard assets will likely be the only thing worth anything.

Appreciation VS Wealth Protection

This idea that Bitcoin, simultaneously, might be better at appreciating than risk assets and better at storing value than other risk-off assets take a lot of pulling apart. It is a concept that is very hard for most people to conceptualize and commonly leads back to misunderstanding Bitcoin's ability to do either. Bitcoin can offer both wealth accumulation and preservation. If you cannot see that, you are probably stuck looking at Bitcoin as a highly volatile tech stock, one that routinely rug-pulls people who don't know when to buy and don't know enough to stomach the volatility to the downside.

How can Bitcoin be an inflation hedge when its price trades like a tech stock? The answer to this question is nuanced. It requires an appreciation for the detrimental long-term effects of constant expansion of the money supply and the power of having an alternative store of financial energy outside that ever-expanding system. Bitcoin's price moves up and down, but over more extended periods, the trend so far has been up only. Today everyone who has held Bitcoin for four years is in profit. Because of the permanently capped supply, the price of Bitcoin attracts and locks capital value from its weaker network alternatives, government fiat currencies. This process can continue to unfold as long as more fragile monetary networks exist. This is why price crashes do not invalidate the Bitcoin thesis because we are observing a real-time process that might take 100 years.

The power and value of Bitcoin in the network are growing by the day. According to 99bitcoins.com, as of November 2022, Bitcoin has been declared dead 464 times. Bitcoin's dramatic boom-bust cycles are not indicative of its inability to store value. We are witnessing the hardening of an emergent asset being battle-tested by a fierce global market. Bitcoin has been banned by countries, has suffered high-profile exchange collapses, birthed stepchild competitor projects, and experienced massive price drawdowns many times. Despite all this, it has yet to collapse and go to zero.

To summarize – Bitcoin traps energy through its capped supply, which in theory, will become much more evident as the network grows and more people understand this. This function simultaneously attracts capital which should cause an ongoing increase in price. The more monetary energy the network stores, the higher the price will go because the circulating supply of Bitcoin will never be more than 21,000,000. Bitcoin offers the simultaneous opportunity to see appreciation in the nominal value of the asset and avoid the devaluation of assets denominated in fiat money. It is a mechanism designed to siphon value away from weaker monetary networks through a free market selection of currency.

So, where might Bitcoin fit into a financial plan? How could we compare Bitcoin to the critical items already bedrock in planning? I want to hand the discussion over to Financial Advisors, which I am not. At the outset of this book, I said my contribution would be to have more advisors take Bitcoin seriously. Also, more advisors think about correctly positioning this asset in a responsible long-term plan.

But I have some thoughts on the matter, from a Bitcoiner's perspective, which I would like to put forward to help nudge the conversation.

Be Responsibly Long

Hopefully, some of you are seeing enough of the picture that you might be thinking about Bitcoin as having the potential to be a core holding – yet without worrying about what part of the existing pie it might come from. I have seen people much brighter than I suggest that a 5% allocation to Bitcoin might outperform the rest of your portfolio over a long enough period. Fidelity has a 2030 price target for Bitcoin of USD 1,000,000. A 50x return on 5% of your portfolio would put your total minimum return, if everything else went to zero, at 150%.

Without getting too frothy about what Bitcoin could do from a price perspective, consider what you have learned about Bitcoin and its potential to continue to attract new capital. Bitcoin is an asset designed to harden as other monies weaken. Suppose that premise proves correct over time; whatever appreciation in price that occurs will likely also be understood as the retained value of the original capital. In that case, this will be obvious to more people if the price appreciation of Bitcoin is accompanied by prolonged high inflation and loss of purchasing power in fiat. Remember that the likelihood of continued debasement of currencies is high, so long-tested ideas about a reasonable return are unlikely to hold over the coming years. Appreciation is a carrot for recommending a Bitcoin investment. Still, it could just as easily be described as a vital part of a defensive strategy for asset protection.

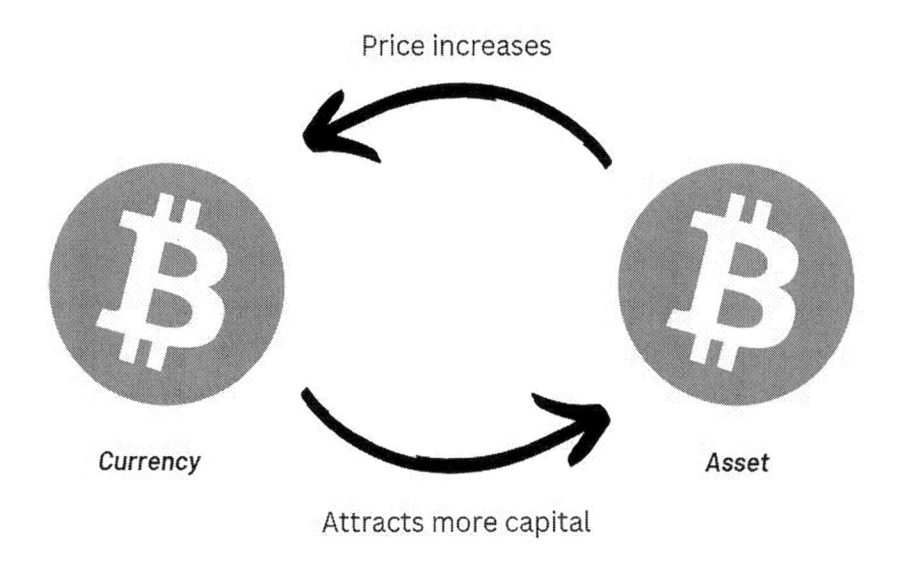

Price increases

Currency → Asset

Attracts more capital

The global debt today is 4x that of the worldwide GDP. This means servicing that debt will require a GDP growth 4 times that of the organic growth rate. If the debt grows at 3%, GDP would need to grow by 12% to keep pace. Given how unlikely this is, it is a fair assumption that countries will have to print money to avoid insolvency. Taking into account all the different types of utility Bitcoin offers; also, the current global economic conditions having some Bitcoin as insurance against something going wrong, is easily worth the risk that somehow Bitcoin the experiment might yet fail.

You have an asset traded this broadly, with this adoption curve profile, operating in favorable market conditions, in a world moving more and more digital every day. That same asset theoretically can appreciate forever. It has a non-zero chance of hitting a 7-figure price tag, which is a 50x return from today. That potential alone is worth being responsibly long for whatever percentage of your portfolio you can stomach.

The key here is having some long-term vision, which is easier said than done when it comes to Bitcoin. How can we expect clients to have a 20-year view of an asset that is not even 20 years old? The answer to this question is education.

Approaching a position in Bitcoin with an extremely long view is the way to remove the emotional highs and lows of price volatility. The validity of the investment thesis in Bitcoin hinges more on Bitcoin's ability to continue to attract more users, the ongoing expansion of the fiat money supply, and the continued integrity of the protocol. So long as all three of those things continue on their current trajectory over a long enough time frame, Bitcoin should continue to outperform.

How Saving In Bitcoin Works

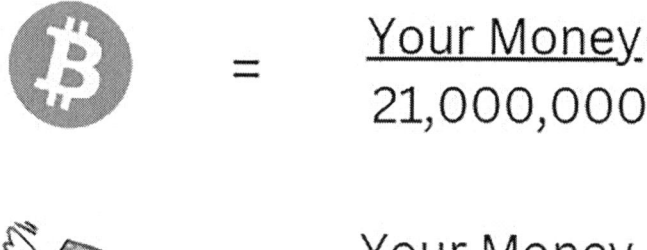

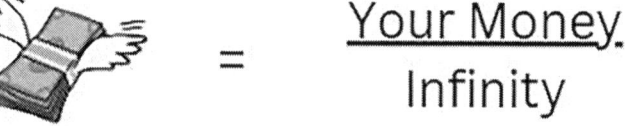

$$\text{₿} = \frac{\text{Your Money}}{21{,}000{,}000}$$

$$\text{💸} = \frac{\text{Your Money}}{\text{Infinity}}$$

Saving Your Money In Bitcoin

Time preference concerning investing in Bitcoin is a concept I was first exposed to in *The Bitcoin Standard*. Time preference measures the urgency for results. The idea of using a currency that is a poor store of value forces those using that currency to have a higher urgency to do something with their money; doing nothing with that money will cost you purchasing power through inflation. Without knowing it, most of our planning ideas revolve around high-time preference. If our money weren't losing value, you would not be under immense pressure for it to grow constantly. While you may not have thought of it this way, financial advisors, perhaps more than any other industry, are slaves to time preference. Customers two years into a 30-year plan to retire are assessing their advisor's competency based on the average returns they achieve in individual years. Time preference is both what would prevent a Bitcoin recommendation and why it is necessary.

We exchange the money we work for into assets that hopefully grow over time. The goal is that appreciating those assets will outpace the diminishing purchasing power of day-to-day things. This is becoming wealthy in the modern world. We are exchanging money for other goods because we inherently know that leaving our money in money is not a viable strategy. Even with interest rates climbing – guaranteed returns on interest certificates may still promise you a number that is half of what inflation is being reported. Think about that; you can sign up for a guaranteed return representing only a 50% loss.

If money were to retain value or become more valuable over time, investment strategies would look much different. This would produce a lower time preference or urgency on returns. Risk profiles would reduce dramatically, and investment in business would need to be much more grounded in reality, instead of the insane forward p/e ratios we have today. Many unviable businesses would have a hard time attracting investors if money could be considered safe not to be invested in anything.

This is the world many of our parents grew up in when the long-term disastrous effects of inflation only started to play out. Our parents were raised by parents who stored physical cash in the house, under a mattress. They could do that because the price of a bottle of coke did not change from 1886 to 1959.[17] This is why my mom, who didn't know much about investing, was still teaching me the value of savings and earning interest when I was 8.

One way to look at an allocation to Bitcoin is to view it as savings. In place of a savings account in cash, your pile of Satoshis would be your money not invested in risky assets like stocks or a rental property. Today the volatility of Bitcoins price in shorter time frames invalidates this argument. However, we are going from 100 million users to over 1 billion. Likely this deviation will change significantly as the total number of users grows exponentially. But saving in fiat is leaving your savings in the hands of those who have already guaranteed they will dilute the value of those savings – it is a crucial mechanism of how the fiat system remains operational.

Fixed Income

My work educating pension plan members got me thinking about many of these ideas in the first place. 2022 has been a catastrophic year for the 60/40 portfolio[18]. Most of the pensions I looked after in

---

[17] "Fixed price of Coca-Cola from 1886 to 1959." Wikipedia. Last modified February 24, 2022. https://en.wikipedia.org/wiki/Fixed_price_of_Coca-Cola_from_1886_to_1959.

[18] "The worst year in U.S. history for the 60/40 portfolio." MarketWatch. September 15, 2021. https://www.marketwatch.com/story/the-worst-year-in-u-s-history-for-the-60-40-portfolio-11663342923.

my practice were set for target date funds, essentially variations of that portfolio.

Bitcoin offers insurance against bonds not performing. Particularly Government bonds, which today are facing some pretty severe headwinds. The evolution of the scale of the debt burden could have a lasting impact on the bond market. Buying Bitcoin out of your fixed-income allocation could be viewed as buying insurance on the possibility that those fixed-income assets do not perform. It can also be considered insurance against the value of your pension benefits being inflated away.

It also needs to be considered instead of interest-bearing assets like GICs.

The argument here is that whatever interest you earn on paper in a currency leaking value at an accelerating rate is not worth anything. It's just rewarding you with a little bit more monopoly money. Suppose the reported inflation rate is double what you are earning on your money in interest. In that case, your defensive strategy costs you much in real wealth.

A former colleague of mine has just received a large payout from selling a business. He immediately put 40% of it into short-term GICs. Standard logic here, stay flexible and earn some money on your money in the meantime. This bright guy is a very successful entrepreneur with a high-level understanding of money.

I explained this concept unsuccessfully to him. It is tough for people to separate the price performance from the store of value. We don't have anything else that does both.

Say, in the very short term, you want to earn money on money you may want to deploy elsewhere soon, Bitcoin might not be a good option.

However, if you are looking for a genuine defense against the loss of purchasing power, storing your money in fiat currency to earn a bit more is not a defense, it's putting a Band-Aid on a gunshot.

Equities

Bitcoin, around USD 20,000, is roughly 3.5x away from its previous all-time price high. The S&P would need to turn 7% for 20 years to accomplish that same return. Bitcoin allocation as a percentage of what you might otherwise put in the market is straightforward. I look at it in two ways.

If you think Bitcoin has any chance to regain its all-time mark over the next 20 years, then it is worth asking, why invest in equities? Maybe it's better to put it this way. Whatever percent chance, or higher, you think is possible for Bitcoin to hit at any point in the future, allocate that amount to Bitcoin.

Instead, if you want to look at specific stocks or funds, ask which other companies or indexes today have a theoretical maximum infinity price. Remember, no one knows the end of Bitcoin's price appreciation. There are 900T of global assets today, and Bitcoin currently represents 300 billion of that total. There is a long, long way up before we must worry about the ceiling.

The world's most significant investment players have barely dipped a toe in Bitcoin. All of them are also hungry for returns and seeking to preserve capital value over time. Say at some future time, sovereign wealth funds, endowments, pension plans, central banks, municipal and provincial governments all have a mere 1% exposure to Bitcoin – we are talking about a market cap growth from hundreds of billions to several trillion if not more.

The Bank of International Settlements has just finished the draft of policy that would allow banks to hold 2% of their balance sheets in Bitcoin, likely by January of 2025.[19] We are not that far away.

Global Assets	Global Debt	Global Real Estate	Global GDP	Gold	Bitcoin
900T USD	400T USD	300T USD	100T USD	15T USD	300B USD
	No Cap			Unknown Max Supply	21 million ever
				0% return over 10 years	

Inheritance

I think Bitcoin makes a lot of sense for testators looking for different ways to pass on wealth to grandchildren. Bitcoin has not existed long enough for us to know. But if Bitcoin were to do a 50x to USD 1,000,000 even over 20 years, that would be an incredible gift to pass down.

A purchase of bitcoin to keep in the family is essentially choosing to store wealth in the asset designed to be the best store of that wealth over time. Bitcoin cannot be confiscated, and there are no tax consequences until disposition. Therefore, bitcoin is an ideal holding for people who are not obsessively watching the price daily. In talking with older people about Bitcoin, I find they understand this concept more easily than younger generations.

---

[19] "Bank of International Settlements' New Policy: Banks to Hold 2% Crypto." CoinGape. August 8, 2021. https://coingape.com/bank-of-international-settlements-new-policy-banks-hold-2percent-crypto/.

Regarding resonating with older people, it is easy for them to see Bitcoin as something their grandkids would value. I have spoken to many older people who are amazed by the idea of Bitcoin but feel it is outside their time horizon. Those same people always ask me whether or not it can be passed down.

There is a different angle to look at this concept. Think what it would mean for younger parents or new grandparents to have more time for this great gift to mature. Buying Bitcoin with your descendants in mind, the younger you are, potentially, the bigger the gift you will be passing on. Suppose Bitcoin continues growing and adopting over a very long time, like 50 or 70 years. In that case, Bitcoin will only become more and more rare. There will always be new Bitcoins being lost. There can never be any more. So as Bitcoin attracts more money and loses more coins, the value of each coin will increase to infinity. For those with a lot of foresight, these are assets you should be planning never to leave your family.

There can only be 21,000,000. So, at what point does having one whole Bitcoin make your family one of the 21,000,000 wealthiest families in the world? I have Bitcoins today I hope never leave my family. I am planning on providing generational wealth for my descendants using Bitcoin today.

Bitcoin ETFs Inside RRSP/ RESP/TFSA/LIRA etc

In the next section, I will compare owning Bitcoin and investing in derivative Bitcoin products. You can currently not hold actual Bitcoin in an RRSP, TFSA, or LIRA, but you can own Bitcoin ETFs. I still think that buying Bitcoin is preferable to having ETFs. However, exposure to Bitcoin through the ETFs inside registered or tax-sheltered products makes a lot of sense to me. From a planning standpoint – Bitcoin is designed to be a value trap for continuously expanding fiat currencies. This makes it an exciting asset to hold inside registered investment vehicles instead of funds or securities.

Having a percentage of your long-term holdings in an ETF that tracks the price of Bitcoin and inside a tax shelter compounds the potential upside Bitcoin offers from a price standpoint. It also removes some of the pressure of short-time performance, and protects saved money against prolonged currency devaluation. The challenge is looking at Bitcoin with a 20 or 30-year time horizon when it is only 14 years old. This is where a good advisor with a sophisticated understanding of what Bitcoin does can help.

Some considerable disadvantages come with the derivative products. Firstly, Bitcoin is an asset that trades continuously, 24-7. You can only trade the ETFs during regular market hours, which makes it less than ideal for anyone looking to trade in and out. You also do not own a claim to any Bitcoin when you invest in a product or Bitcoin fund. This obviously confers none of the benefits of actual Bitcoin, such as borderless, uncensorable wealth that nobody can confiscate.

There is also the potential issue of the ethics under which those funds are operated. As 2022 draws to a close, the Greyscale Bitcoin trust has a widening discount between the unit price and the price of Bitcoin. It's not an ETF, but the trust refuses to be transparent about which Bitcoin wallet holds the 600,000+ Bitcoin they purport to have. The Bitcoin network's transparency will pose problems for traditional financial services offerings where Bitcoin is the underlying asset. They will need to offer the transparency expected based on what the technology enables. Failure to do so could cause a critical collapse of market confidence.

So far, Greyscale's refusal to share the wallet address has the market speculating they do not actually have the Bitcoins they say they do. This is hard to believe, but trust, even in institutional Bitcoin products, has been rattled in 2022. There is no alternative from a safety-of-funds perspective to a client cold-storing their own Bitcoin.

As a Corporate Asset

I think there are a couple of exciting ways to look at this. I believe this idea makes a ton of sense for business owners – particularly those looking for extra ways to invest inside their corps.

Say you think of Bitcoin as digital property. Buying some Bitcoin is potentially a simple alternative for a company that is considering investing in physical real estate. Bitcoin is simple to purchase, does not finance, and is just as easy to dispose of at the time of sale.

Privately held companies won't necessarily need to worry about the impairment that might come with Bitcoin's short-term ups and downs. Owners who understand the concept of Bitcoin as a corporate asset, beyond being an investment, could benefit tremendously from tax-preferred gains should Bitcoin continue to outperform.

This is a rehashing of the dual-purpose concept I discussed previously. In terms of potentially protecting the value of retained earnings inside a corporation, Bitcoin also has exciting potential. The volatility prevents businesses from holding working capital in Bitcoin in case it might need deployment on short notice. However, to store retained earnings not required immediately, it is something to consider.

There are public companies already employing this strategy. Tesla (TSLA) made headlines by announcing in the spring of 2020 that they would start holding Bitcoin on their balance sheet. Today Micro Strategies (MSTR) has the largest corporate Bitcoin treasury disclosed among public companies. MSTR has performed very well, even during the Bitcoin downturn outperforming most other tech stocks and the indexes.

Bitcoin Instead of Real Estate

Since I poked fun at real estate at the start of the book, I have been waiting to return to this topic. I find it funny that the same people who think Bitcoin is 'culty' often consider die-hard believers that you will never lose money in real estate as entirely sane.

Bitcoin is already dramatically outperforming real estate, albeit with vastly greater volatility. Ironically part of the reason for the difference in the relative volatility of these assets is the percentage of each market obsessed with price. Say everyone who owned a home was checking the price movement of their home every day or even multiple times a day. The psychological stress of owning a home (given that it is, for 99% of owners, their most significant asset and liability) would be too high to bear. Instead, homeowners will obsessively look at their Bitcoin price, which is probably <1% of their net worth, and decide to sell when they are down 50% because the risk is too high.

This topic, in particular, is fair game for me. As I stated earlier, I made a conscious decision to exit real estate in favor of Bitcoin in 2021. Canadian real estate has been mostly up only now for 20+ years with various degrees of ridiculous depending on the local market. Some people are buying in now, expecting this run to happen again. They are assuming that the market and wages will somehow permit this type of long-term price appreciation to occur again. I can't imagine a riskier bet.

The problem with real estate is we need house prices to go up forever. For most people, paying off a home in their lifetime has become the only path to long-term financial freedom. Homes have become our financial batteries because they are better stores of value than the money we use. Over the last 20 and 50 years, they have appreciated more than the cost of everything else. Real estate has become the backbone of the inflationary delusion of everyone 'getting richer' as the denomination of assets in funny money goes up over time. Assessing the long-term viability of this system begs the question: where will the buyers continue to come from to prop up the price growth as the percentage of household income allocated towards your residence is already an unsustainable portion of the total?

I understand why this strategy has become a pillar of basic finance. For most people, it's a sad reality that they feel no good choice exists. If you are buying a house as a lifestyle choice to own, that is a choice I respect entirely. Also, you can't live inside your Bitcoin.

I am challenging the view that it is a no-brainer to think real estate is a superior investment to Bitcoin. In my opinion, the only scenario where real estate outperforms Bitcoin over the next 20 years is if Bitcoin somehow breaks.

Bitcoin has a much larger market of buyers, is more liquid, and has a much larger potential market cap relative to its current market cap. It is owned outright, so it is less sensitive to financing costs. Bitcoin requires no maintenance or capital improvements. The value of bitcoin is less subjective. No one can foreclose your bitcoin, and you do not have to pay a tax yearly just for the right to own it. Real estate is losing value in Bitcoin at an incredible rate. According to pricedinbitcoin21.com, the mean price of a used home in America in 2012 was USD 221,700 or

BTC 44,340. On January 1, 2022, the price of that house had risen to USD 423,400, BTC 9.15. I don't expect the next ten years to produce the same astronomical difference in performance. Still, I think it's fair to say that as asset classes, they have almost nothing in common from a realistic appraisal of what the next 10 or 20 years will look like.

There are two scenarios where I strongly feel Bitcoin makes more sense than real estate. Young people are starting to save a down payment to enter the market, and investors or entities are looking to invest in real estate to diversify through secondary properties. Ignoring all the nuances, I will touch on each very quickly. Properly addressing this topic in depth would be an entire chapter, which I will save for a future book.

Young people looking to enter the market with minimum down payments are taking the path of maximum pain, particularly as interest rates climb. The early terms in their mortgages are almost entirely interest. Their first home will only work out if they can sell it to someone else at a higher price. Putting that same down payment in Bitcoin instead allows them to let Bitcoin, the asset, do the work appreciating relative to real estate. Today, it might purchase an entire Bitcoin, and we could easily see the day shortly when one Bitcoin will buy an entire home.

Secondary properties combine all the worst aspects of the asset class (risk of bad tenants, need for maintenance, unfavorable tax status). These aspects come as a trade for the income a rental generates and the feeling of security in the track record of the asset class. I have spoken to many people who own more than one property and refuse to buy even one Bitcoin. There is a comfort level here that will equalize for most the longer Bitcoin survives and the more established it becomes. The difference is that this strategy's opportunity will have diminished considerably by that time. Again, whether as a planner you buy into this idea or not – part of what I want to do is expose those helping everyday people make these decisions to different ideas.

Don't Be Peter Zeihan

"Bitcoin will not only go to zero, it will probably go to negative because in a world with carbon taxes you will have to take into account the energy it took to produce it"

Peter Zeihan is an American Author and Academic who appeared on Joe Rogan in January of 2023 in an interview that went viral based on some strong "bitcoin has failed" statements he made, including the claim that at $16,000 bitcoin had another $17,000 down to go. That interview is definitely worth a watch. One of his most brazen opinions voiced that day was the claim that the permanent cap of the supply of bitcoin would prohibit it from ever being a functional means of exchange in a global economy that is designed to expand. Basically the idea here is that economic output grows, so by extension it makes sense that the money supply must grow along with it.

If you haven't got this part yet, the idea is we have either finite stuff and infinite money or we have finite stuff and finite money. Jeff Booth does a great job explaining how technology by nature is deflationary, driving production cost down, and that prices should come down as a result of deflation in a world of finite money. Zeihan is looking at the fixed supply of money as something that will lead to a lack of liquidity inevitably drying up the economy - this is because he does not understand bitcoins divisibility. Bitcoin can be endlessly subdivided, there is no worry of running out. Bitcoins hardcap creates a point of reference for true price signals to come through the market. Jeff Booth devoted an entire book to this discussion if you are interested in the deep dive.

For the purposes of this segment, I am simply noting that there are some very smart, high profile thinkers, with big platforms - who simply have not grasped bitcoin basics. It's easy to decide why bitcoin can't replace traditional financial instrument x, without really looking at the counter arguments. Zeihan happens to be a great example of this.

Some Common Questions

"If you are not long Bitcoin, you're exposed to an incredible short position on what could be the best performing asset of this century." Greg Foss

Custodial Bitcoin VS Non-Custodial

Precisely who has control over purchased bitcoin is an important concept to understand. Custodial Bitcoin is when someone lets a third party store their bitcoin for them. Today these are often bitcoin exchanges, and they could very well be commercial banks in the future. A common phrase among the Bitcoin community is 'not your keys, not your coins.' When you do not personally possess bitcoin, you do not own bitcoin. You own an IOU to bitcoin. Most Canadians are aware of the Quadriga scandal in Vancouver a few years ago. I get asked about scams and Quadriga often. The simplest answer is that self-custody is a crucial aspect of owning bitcoin.

Storing your own bitcoin is a feature, not a bug, of the Bitcoin network. Self-custody represents a new way of doing things for many. Still, it is a vital component of the security offered by the network. For people who still do not view banks as a burden or point of friction, the concept of being in charge of the custody of your assets can be a cause of concern. This is another point of access where financial advisors will eventually understand and be able to speak to self-custody. This is a natural and likely progression of how financial advice will change to keep pace with the evolution of the tools. Financial advice, in general, and what is required to be current will continue to evolve. The trend toward understanding self-custody is unlikely to go away.

Bitcoin VS Gold

Much has been written about the standard comparison between Bitcoin and gold as stores of value. Gold and Bitcoin are different assets designed to do different things, and both are worth owning. Rather than explain in detail, I will summarize the key arguments for why Bitcoin is a superior asset.

Bitcoin is superior to gold in that it is more portable. You can send bitcoin anywhere in the world in minutes. It is impossible to prevent bitcoin from crossing a border. The bitcoin market is more liquid and easier to access. It trades 24-7, and you only need an internet connection to sell it. Bitcoin is more uniform and divisible than gold; each has 100,000,000 identical subunits called Satoshi's. There are no grades of bitcoin. Bitcoin is more storable than gold. You do not need a vault to store large amounts of bitcoin, just a cell phone or a USB. Bitcoin is scarcer than gold. In the spring, a gold deposit was discovered in Africa that is potentially the size of all the currently mined gold in the world. We do not know the maximum supply of gold, but we know precisely how much bitcoin there will ever be. We don't even know how much gold the Federal Reserve holds because they refuse to conduct a transparent audit. The paper market has destroyed price signals for gold. The paper bitcoin market will cease to exist by around 2027 at the current rate of bitcoin leaving exchanges today. Finally, as an asset class, Bitcoin is 30 to 50 times smaller than gold. At a USD 20,000 price, bitcoin has a total value of roughly USD 300B. Gold is somewhere between USD 10-15T. From a potential price appreciation standpoint, bitcoin becoming even 50% of the size of gold as an asset would mean USD 5-7T stored in the network. This would catapult prices north of USD 300k.

Gold offers scarcity to a lesser degree, is a store of value, and has a several thousand-year track record. However, it does not have a network effect because of its physical qualities.

Bitcoin VS the Bitcoin ETFs

In Canada today, we have a few ETF options that track bitcoin's spot price. These offer an opportunity to get bitcoin exposure for investors who don't want to buy actual bitcoin. They also allow bitcoin exposure in an RRSP, TFSA, LIRA, or possibly even a pension.

Investing in the bitcoin ETF, you only get exposure to the price (which can be good and bad). However, at the expense of being able to trade only during regular hours, Monday to Friday. Those watching the price of bitcoin crash over a weekend will have to wait until Monday morning to panic-sell their bitcoin ETF. Bitcoin itself is trading 24-7. Hence, you are limited in your ability to settle in and out of a position in the short term.

With ETFs, you get none of the other benefits of actual bitcoin. They have a place, but my opinion is custodial bitcoin holdings should be the priority. Understanding bitcoin well enough to stop caring about short-term volatility generally takes a long time. For this reason, I believe ETFs can be harder psychologically to hold.

Bitcoin VS Cryptocurrencies

The book on the emerging digital asset space is in its very early stages. Many other cryptocurrencies, including the Ether token on the Ethereum network, have outperformed bitcoin as an investment in shorter timeframes. However, every other cryptocurrency is a centralized project with a public team behind it. This means they are businesses with specific motivations, and many of them may yet turn out to be unregistered securities. Only a handful (all offshoots of the Bitcoin protocol) have the same hard money principles around total supply. The rest of them are inflationary and no different than fiat money.

Cryptocurrencies may continue to be high-performing investments. However, none offer bitcoin's decentralization, hard principles, and network effect. They commonly get lumped together by outsiders. But it is more accurate to consider Bitcoin entirely separate from the rest of the cryptocurrency space and orders of magnitude safer from a long-term investment standpoint.

Do I need to Buy a Whole Bitcoin?

Hopefully, this is obvious at this point, but it often comes up. As Bitcoin is divisible by eight decimal places, anyone can buy any micro amount of bitcoin. This makes it ideal for people in poorer parts of the world to accumulate.

With only 21,000,000 available ever, there are nowhere near enough bitcoins for most people even to aspire to own one. Among Bitcoin investors, the term 'whole-coiner' describes that group of people. Over time, that club could prove to be very small.

Dollar Cost Average or Lump Sum Purchase?

This is another question I get asked all the time. Despite its incredible track record of price appreciation, bitcoin is highly volatile – leaving many considering a purchase unsure about when to start. This leads to another typical conversation I have where interested people are waiting for an even better price.

The media focuses on bitcoin's boom/bust cycles to scare new entrants away by pumping the hype when the price rises and focusing endlessly on negative news when the opposite occurs. If you think people get panicked about financial news on TV regarding regular assets, wait until you sell someone bitcoin.

The bitcoin sentiment extremes are so intense that buying the bottom is unrealistic for anyone not already immersed in the concept. Investors should understand this and plan accordingly. This can be a lump sum purchase for those who are ok with the idea that there might be a lower price at some point in the future.

For those less interested in taking the plunge, DCA can be a powerful tool for accumulating bitcoin because it takes care of the need to worry about timing the market. It removes the anxiety around whether or not the price could go dramatically down or up in the near future.

Those who diligently DCA into bitcoin have been rewarded. A weekly purchase over the past four years would today be up over 250%. That takes the downturn over the past 12 months into account.

The alternative perspective is that should Bitcoin ever hit an astronomical price tag in the future, whether your average purchase price is USD 22,000 or USD 24,000 will probably not matter all that much.

There is an excellent tool for calculating the return on DCA strategies for Bitcoin; find it at www.dcabtc.com

Don't Be Jim Rickards

"You can take the orange pill now, or be forced to take the orange suppository later." Knut Svanholm

I love Jim Rickards. I read every book he puts out and will listen to any podcast that has him on as a guest. He's educated, well spoken, and his books are thoroughly researched. His viewpoints are an intersection of economics, history, and political science which appeal to my academic background. He is a highly respected thinker, having served as an advisor to the Pentagon and the Department of Defense. In spite of all this, Jim is probably the worst informed "Bitcoin expert" I have ever come across. Jim claims to have studied Bitcoin for over a thousand hours dating back to 2010. He certainly knows the key terms and talks confidently about the subject in detail, regularly sharing his misunderstandings with great conviction. When it comes to Bitcoin, it's not like Jim is confused about a few unimportant details. His misunderstandings are so egregious it's become hard for me to take any of his other scholarly works seriously. How anyone known for academic research could study Bitcoin for 10 years and remain ignorant about basic concepts is impossible to explain. To be this wrong about so many different aspects of how bitcoin works, the only explanation is that he is either the most hard-headed scholar alive or he is doing it on purpose. In May of 2022 Jim participated in part 2 of Stansberry's Bitcoin vs Gold debate speaking on behalf of gold. Here are a collection of incorrect ideas he advanced just in that one interview.

Bitcoin is not durable because all you need to do is turn off the electricity and it's gone. While this statement does possibly apply to local areas, the idea that globally we will ever be without electricity is not one I will be betting on. There may be scenarios where prolonged local power outages might make using Bitcoin difficult, but it does not need to be mined locally. So long as cellphones and local internet service are working bitcoin can be exchanged. This argument really only holds water if there is a prolonged global power outage. If that scenario were to occur, it would be from something cataclysmic. The Bitcoin network would likely be the least of our worries. Furthermore, Jim implies that bitcoin might actually cease to exist without electricity. Electricity is a core requirement to access the bitcoin network but without it, so long as the network is running elsewhere, the records of your bitcoin transactions remain unaffected.

Bitcoin is not portable because the Canadian government froze Bitcoins in February of 2022. Bitcoin can only be frozen when custodied by a third party. It is more accurate to say exchange accounts or bitcoins custodied by third parties were frozen. Bitcoin custodied in a private wallet cannot be frozen by anyone, including governments.

Criminal investigators can trace the entire history of a particular bitcoin. The history of a bitcoin address is simple to find, and it is equally simple to track a history of transactions of other addresses interacting with it. On the Bitcoin network following the flow of funds is straight forward. There is no type of data available to distinguish one bitcoin from another. The transparency of transaction history is a positive, and the network was not designed to be primarily used by criminals and terrorists. The fact that Bitcoin transactions can be tracked does not mean it cannot be money.

Each bitcoin has its own digital footprint. Bitcoins do not have serial numbers. In fact, bitcoins do not technically even exist. The network is a record of transactions which actually measure the amount of bitcoin that weren't spent in a transaction as a way to infer how much bitcoin an address has. This is called unspent transaction output or UTXO. UTXO is a strange concept for newcomers, but anyone 1000 hours of study into the subject will certainly have at least come across the topic.

Bitcoins scarcity is a fatal flaw. According to Jim the world could never run on a currency with a finite supply. This opinion shows almost no understanding of exactly how divisible bitcoin is. There are quadrillions of Satoshi's available to be exchanged in spite of whatever the total number of lost bitcoin, or the fact that in over 100 years from now there will be no more new bitcoin to be mined. The price of a whole bitcoin can easily rise to a point where a single Satoshi is a meaningful amount of money. Further decimal places could eventually be added if required.

We may never get to the last mined Bitcoin because each math problem becomes harder than the one before and the amount of computing power and processing power and electricity that you need to do one more hash as you get toward the final Bitcoin go up and at some point, the reward won't be worth it.

The math problems in bitcoin mining do not get progressively harder in a linear fashion. Mining difficulty constantly adjusts to match the amount the effort being expended mining. This is a key innovation in the system, designed to prevent bitcoins from being mined too fast but also to make sure the economics of mining make as much sense as possible. While it is true that the electricity and computing power required to mine will likely rise over time, they can only do so in concert with whatever commensurate fees make mining financially viable. Because miners are rewarded in bitcoin the only way the network functions is if the rewards over time are higher than the costs. As bitcoins become more rare and more expensive to mine, the rewards will appreciate appropriately or, the number of miners will decrease to a point where the difficulty drops and it becomes viable again. The system is constantly adjusting, and it will continue to constantly adjust even when there is only one bitcoin left to be mined.

The Bitcoin community can get together and change the 21,000,000 cap. This battle has already been fought and lost. Over the course of the mid-2010s various factions in the Bitcoin community proposed several changes to the amount of data held on each block. This is essential Bitcoin history and was captured in detail in a book called The Blocksize Wars. It is true that anyone can change the Bitcoin code, but the only way actual change happens to Bitcoin is if everyone including miners, node operators, and users migrate to the new blockchain. There will never be community agreement to dilute the supply of Bitcoin, or to do anything that could potentially degrade its value. That ship has sailed.

Bitcoin can be impounded, interdicted, erased. None of these statements are true for Bitcoin. The keys to a bitcoin wallet can be memorized and stored in your head. While countries have banned Bitcoin, bans in practice are a little bit like banning talking. It's a software that connects users directly without an intermediary. For people who already have Bitcoin, preventing them from sending that bitcoin to an address hoping to receive it is impossible. The only way to erase a bitcoin would be to take control of 51% of the network, a theoretical scenario which is already such a monumental effort that even the United States Government would be hard pressed to muster the resources to do it. In theory it would be much simpler for governments to destroy Bitcoin than ban it. So it is reasonable to infer that the 51% attack would likely already have happened if it were feasible and the fact that it has not is evidence of how hard it is to execute.

Bitcoin is a casino chip. Not a useful form of money, just gambling. I have moral/ethical objections to Bitcoin. Even if you are among the world's slowest readers, I can't imagine getting to this point in the book has taken you 1000 hours. I would hope by now, after just a few hours of introductory reading, even if you are not clamoring to buy your first bitcoin that you can appreciate Bitcoin is much more than casino currency.

Jim's perspective, if this is how he truly feels about Bitcoin, demonstrates a collection of basically all the mistakes I have tried to address or recommend avoiding. He claims to have researched for over 1000 hours and still holds the opinion that Bitcoin is a worthless, speculative, potentially immoral monetary network. In all of his studies he has failed to grasp basic concepts of how the network operates, and the complex mechanisms that confer its unique attributes. I can't imagine studying anything for that long, and still being fundamentally uninformed about the basics of the subject. In this respect, Jim is the quintessential person to avoid being when assessing Bitcoin.

The Case for Further Bitcoin Education

"Those having torches will pass them on to others." – Plato

I believe in advisors, and I'm excited for the day when the average person asks their advisor to help them understand Bitcoin. I want to congratulate you for taking a first step towards a better understanding of Bitcoin.

My true hope here is that by now, you are at least encouraged to dive deeper down the rabbit hole and start learning more. I know people will eventually want to talk to their trusted advisor about Bitcoin. It's your job to have enough information to give them the right advice.

Advisors will need to adopt new ideas at a growing pace in the coming years to stay relevant and keep pace with the financial evolution that decentralization will bring. Expect your role and the strategies and products you recommend to change as well. Expect Bitcoin to be a part of your future, helping people on their financial journeys. You may even have to convince clients to look at Bitcoin someday. By then, you'll know enough about it that you'll feel the same satisfaction as today when you convince a client to make an intelligent, more time-tested decision.

Should you be looking for your next step already, I recommend some of my favorite Bitcoin books for you to learn from the masters.

The Price of Tomorrow – Jeff Booth

The Bitcoin Standard – Saifedean Ammous

Bitcoin: Everything Divided by 21 Million – Knut Svanholm

The 7th Property – Eric Yakes

The Blocksize War – Jonathan Bier

Why Buy Bitcoin – Andy Edstrom

21 Lessons: What I've Learned from Falling Down the Bitcoin Rabbit Hole – Gigi

Other Bitcoin minds whom I routinely seek out are Alex Gladstein, Carl Menger, Greg Foss, Marty Bent, Michael Saylor, Preston Pysh, and Robert Breedlove. However, my list is always growing, and I constantly find bright ideas that further challenge what I think I already know.

Consuming Bitcoin ideas coming from those committed to Bitcoin is important- even if your only goal is to form a neutral opinion. Keep in mind that traditional financial institutions, legacy investors, and legacy financial media are unlikely to present unbiased information on the subject. Because Bitcoin has no official spokesperson to defend itself, fair rebuttals can truly only come from those committed to the idea.

Advisors have a responsibility to help their clients navigate the financial gauntlet of life. A vital part of that is assisting people in avoiding pitfalls and mistakes. Do the homework on Bitcoin today to make your own informed opinion about whether avoiding a position in Bitcoin now is a mistake you don't want your trusting clients to make.

Thank you for reading.

Manufactured by Amazon.ca
Bolton, ON